DEDICATION

To all the change makers in the world, the ones who refuse to settle for 'how it's always been,' who stand tall when it would be easier to shrink, who speak truth when silence would be safer, and who dare to believe that their voice, their work, and courage can spark transformation.

This book is for you.

May your light never dim, and may your ripple become a wave.

"Every message shared in courage becomes a ripple that touches shores far beyond what the messenger can see."

- From The Changemakers

CHANGE
MAKERS
ENTREPRENEURS WITH A MISSION
VOICES WITH A MESSAGE
THE PROFESSIONAL SPEAKERS ACADEMY
UNLEASHING 17 VOICES, 17 JOURNEYS.
ONE RIPPLE EFFECT THAT WILL
TRANSFORM YOUR LIFE & BUSINESS.

CONTENTS

INTRODUCTION

The Changemakers:
Entrepreneurs With a Mission, Voices With a Message.

In every generation, there rises a collective of bold souls who refuse to blend in - visionaries who challenge the status quo, break ceilings, and turn their personal trials into platforms of transformation.
The Changemakers is a testament to that spirit. It's not just a book; it's a movement - a gathering of 17 powerful voices from **The Professional Speakers Academy,** each one forged in the fire of experience and refined through the pursuit of purpose.

These are not ordinary entrepreneurs. They are builders of legacies, creators of movements, and carriers of messages that matter.
Each has faced their own crucible - moments that tested their resilience, questioned their identity, and demanded their growth. Yet, through those moments, they discovered a truth that unites them all: business is not just about profit; it's about purpose.

Within these pages, you'll walk alongside founders, mentors, speakers, and thought leaders who turned pain into platforms, and setbacks into setups for something far greater. You'll encounter stories that will stir your courage, strategies that will stretch your thinking, and insights that will remind you that transformation isn't reserved for the elite - it's the birthright of anyone willing to rise.

Each author in this collection has not only built a business but also embraced a mission - to influence, to inspire, and to ignite change in others. Their words are raw, real, and refreshingly authentic. They'll take you behind the glossy highlight reels and into the gritty reality of entrepreneurship - the long nights, the self-doubt, the divine nudges, and the relentless pursuit of impact. But this isn't merely a compilation of success stories. **It's a ripple effect in print.** Every chapter is a spark - an invitation for you to reflect, realign, and reignite your own mission.

Whether you're a seasoned entrepreneur, a leader in transition, or someone standing on the edge of a new beginning, this book is your call to action: to step into your voice, own your message, and make your mark.

The world doesn't change just through titles or talks, it changes through action. And in Changemakers, you'll find 17 action takers who are not only talking the talk but walking the walk - of what happens when courage meets calling.

So, take a deep breath, turn the page, and prepare to be moved. Because once you hear these voices, you won't see business - or yourself - the same way again.

This is the Changemakers.
17 Voices. 17 Journeys. One ripple effect that can transform your life and business.

CHAPTER 1
FROM PAIN TO PURPOSE

To be successful you MUST give up the need for approval from others, and trust yourself.

- Andy Harrington

It's November 2012, and I'm standing at the back of the ballroom in London's Grosvenor House Hotel. Crystal chandeliers shimmer above a crowd of the wealthy and well-connected, but my focus is elsewhere.

From my vantage point, I can see him - larger than life even while seated. Ten years I've waited for this moment. Dreamed of it. Doubted it. Fought for it. And now, here I am.

On stage, comedian Ruby Wax is warming up the audience, her trademark wit cutting through the air. To her left and right stand four members of the U.S. Secret Service, their dark suits and earpieces making the scene look like a movie set.

"Ladies and gentlemen," Ruby announces in that unmistakable voice, "please welcome to the stage, former President of the United States of America, Bill Clinton."

Three hundred people rise to their feet in thunderous applause. But I stay seated. My mind isn't on Clinton. It's on the man sitting at the top table - six foot seven, broad-shouldered, unmistakable. Tony Robbins. This is it. The moment to end a cycle that began more than a decade ago.

As Clinton speaks, my mind drifts back to where it all started - the Old Bailey, London, November 2001.

The Beginning of Change

I'm sitting in the gallery of Court No. 4, looking down on the dark oak panels, the barristers in wigs, and formality of the space. The air is thick with tension.

In the dock sits a young woman I'm close to - early twenties, small, fragile-looking, but brave beyond belief. She's giving evidence against the man who violated her trust and shattered her sense of safety.

As she finishes, her counsel asks quietly, "Is there anything you'd like to add?"

She grips the rail, trembling but determined. "Yes," she says. "I'm going to say something I didn't have the courage to say before."

The courtroom stills.

"No longer am I going to believe it was my fault. No longer am I going to keep your secret. It's over. The truth is out."

The words echo around the chamber, and in that instant, I realise courage isn't the absence of fear - it's action in spite of it.

The verdict comes later: guilty. Relief floods through us both, but what follows isn't peace. It's silence - the kind that fills a house when someone you love has shut down completely.

Despite running a £21 million recruitment company at the time, I felt utterly powerless. All the money in the world meant nothing when I couldn't help the person I loved to find herself again.

When I checked her into the Priory Clinic, the consultant said she was clinically depressed and prescribed medication. But deep down, I knew pills weren't the answer.

A Late-Night Spark

One night, exhausted and desperate, I flicked on the TV. A late night infomercial caught my attention - an American giant named Anthony Robbins was talking about mastering your emotions, transforming your life, and reclaiming your power.

Something about his conviction pierced the fog. I picked up the phone and called the number on the screen.

Changemakers

"Thank you for calling the Anthony Robbins Companies," said a cheerful voice. "This is Marshonda - how may I help you?"

Forty minutes later, I'd enrolled in Tony's Mastery University. I didn't know exactly what I was buying - only that I was buying hope.

Against all advice, I checked her out of hospital, and we flew to Florida for *Unleash the Power Within.*

Thousands of people filled the arena. Tony stormed the stage, booming: *"You already have the power to change!"*

That night, my partner was one of those chosen for a live intervention in front of 5,000 people. I held my breath as Tony worked with her, guiding her from pain to laughter, from despair to joy - right there on stage.

In that single session, everything changed. She realised she could choose meaning over memory, focus over fear. And I realised something too: I was meant to help others find that same power.

A thought whispered inside me: "Maybe that's why you're here, Andy. Maybe it's meant to be you on that stage too."

But almost as soon as I heard it, I dismissed it. "Don't be ridiculous. Who's going to listen to you?"

A Date with Destiny

Months later, we attended Tony's Date with Destiny event in South Carolina. On the final day, participants were asked to pair up and hold eye contact - to truly see one another.

I hesitated. Everyone quickly found a partner - except me.
And one other person.

Tony Robbins.

When our eyes met, I gestured awkwardly, asking if he'd partner with me. To my shock, he nodded.

We sat opposite each other for what felt like forever – five minutes of silence that said everything.

Tears welled up. I thought of what his work had done for us, and how, through him, we'd found hope again. To my surprise, I saw tears in his eyes too.

In that moment, I made a decision that changed my life.

Even though I wasn't yet a speaker, author, or coach, I vowed to learn, grow, and one day inspire others the way he had inspired me. And perhaps – just perhaps – share a stage with him.

Ten Years Later

July 2011. Backstage at London's Excel Centre.

Nine thousand people fill the arena. I can hear the low hum of excitement beyond the curtain.

Beside me stands Beckie – the woman who would soon become my wife – whispering, "This is your moment. You've got this."

I step onto the stage to a roar of applause. I'm about to speak alongside Tony Robbins.

It's hard to describe what that moment felt like – the full circle of a decade's journey. The failures, the rebuilding, the doubts, the grit. All of it leading here.

Since then, I've shared stages with world leaders, entrepreneurs, and icons - from Sir Richard Branson to Robert Kiyosaki, from Steve Wozniak to Bill Clinton.

And that brings me back to this ballroom in 2012.

Clinton finishes his speech. The audience rises again. My heart races. I stride toward Tony, tap him on the shoulder, and as he turns to face me, I find myself once again looking into those same eyes that once changed everything.

"Hi Tony," I say. "I'm Andy Harrington. We've shared the stage a few times, but I wanted to thank you - because ten years ago, you inspired me to change my life."

We shake hands. And in that instant, I realise: the cycle is complete. I am no longer the student seeking change - I am the changemaker.

Why You Should Read This Book

Every great transformation begins with a decision - a line in the sand where you say, enough is enough.

For me, that decision began in a courtroom and ended on a stage. For you, it might begin on this page.

This book, Changemakers, is written for those who know they're meant for more. People who have overcome challenges, gained wisdom, and now feel a calling to use their story - not as a wound, but as a weapon for good.

Because the truth is:

Right now, there are people in the world who want to know what you already know - and they're waiting for you to show up.

Every one of the changemakers you'll meet in these pages has walked through their own fire. They didn't just learn something - they lived it. They found meaning in their struggle, turned it into a method, and now use it to transform lives.

In these chapters, you'll learn how they did it - their step-by-step frameworks, mindsets, and models that help people change faster, go further, and live fuller.

You'll discover how to:

Turn your life lessons into lasting impact.

Transform your expertise into a real business that serves others.

Build influence, income, and inner fulfilment - all at once.

And as you do, you'll see that **you too are a changemaker in waiting.** You don't need letters after your name. You don't need to be "qualified" by anyone but life itself. Your qualification is your experience, your empathy, and your energy to serve.

We live in an era where your message can reach millions from your phone, your stage, or your story. The question is: will you use what happened to you to make something happen through you? Because this isn't just a book - it's an invitation.

An invitation to rise. To lead. To use your life to light the way for others. If you're ready to make a difference - in your business, your relationships, your community, or even your own sense of purpose - then turn the page.

Changemakers

Your story is waiting to be written. And who knows? One day, perhaps someone will read your chapter... and find in it the spark that changes everything.

ANDY HARRINGTON

CHANGE
MAKERS
ENTREPRENEURS WITH A MISSION
VOICES WITH A MESSAGE
THE PROFESSIONAL SPEAKERS ACADEMY
UNLEASHING 17 VOICES, 17 JOURNEYS.
ONE RIPPLE EFFECT THAT WILL
TRANSFORM YOUR LIFE & BUSINESS.

CHAPTER 2

IT'S NEVER TOO LATE TO BE GREAT

REDISCOVERING IDENTITY, PURPOSE AND JOY

"It's only too late
if you've taken your
last breath!"

– Ali Gordon

• • •

Have you ever felt your identity, purpose, or joy quietly slip away as you pass through life?

Have you ever wondered if maybe your chance to start over has also passed you by?

If so, then this chapter is for you!

I want to start by reminding you - you are not too old,
and it is not too late.

God sees you. He knows your story, and He can breathe new life into your dreams. Even now, there's a path ahead filled with meaning, hope, and joy, just waiting for you to take the first step; even if you cannot see it or feel it right now.

For me, my journey began the moment I realised my lowest point wasn't the end, it was the place God chose to start something new.

From aloha to ashes

I feel it in my bones; life is about to change forever.

Eighteen months of training in Hawaii, Plumeria on the breeze, waves on the shore... then six months in Papua New Guinea as a Medical Missionary. My dream is finally real, I can taste the salty air, feel the promise ahead.

Then, in a heartbeat, it shatters. After just six weeks, I'm asked to leave.

The colour drains from my world. Confidence, hope, belief in the future, all vanish, leaving me in the shadow of the life I thought was mine.

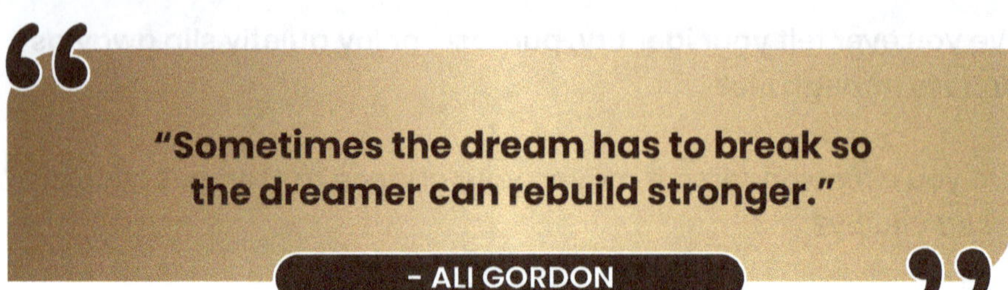

When the wheel isn't mine!

Back in Madrid, I'm fighting to hold myself together, desperate for help. I know I need professional support, but doors slam shut. Calls go unanswered. Referrals drag on for months. My life is crumbling while the system shrugs.

I tell myself to be patient. It takes time, they say. But my patience is gone. My mind spirals, each day another brick in the wall trapping me inside my own head.

When I finally enter The Priory in London, I think, "At last, I'm in charge of my healing!".

But I'm not!

The steering wheel of my life has been taken, and not by choice.

Home Front Heartaches

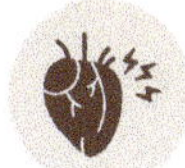

If you've ever been in crisis, you'll know, family can be both your greatest comfort and your greatest challenge.

Mine is in open conflict. Arguments over who is "right," who "understands" me best, me or them; whose opinion "matters."

Instead of focusing on healing, I'm fielding emotional grenades from the people I love. It's exhausting to be in the middle of a war I never asked for.

Is love for me?

In my darkest moments, I wonder if God has abandoned me.

If He truly loves me, why am I still in pain? Why has He allowed my dreams to shatter? Maybe I'm not worth rescuing. Maybe I'm too broken.

If you've ever felt unseen, unheard, or forgotten by people or God, you'll understand the weight of these questions.

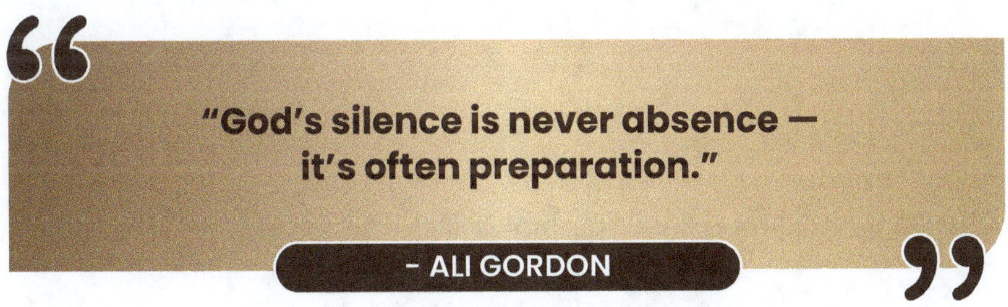

A messenger in disguise the day choice disappeared

Then comes the gut punch!

My voluntary status at The Priory is removed. Simply because I am a little too keen to leave the hospital to be able to make my own rules again! I am officially "sectioned" under the Mental Health Act (1983).

In plain English? I cannot leave, even if I want to.

I am now terrified! Totally, physically, spiritually terrified. This is my worst-case scenario. All I wanted to do was go home, but instead I feel trapped with even less control than before!

And then... he appears, "the man with the kind eyes".
He doesn't lecture or judge. He just sits with me in a disused corridor and truly sees me. His calm presence steadies me.

Later, staff insist no one was there with me on the security camera footage, but I know he was real. An angel. A whisper from God, "You are not abandoned. I am here."

God Has a Plan

Meeting "the man with the kind eyes" changes me. I see that no matter how lost I feel, a turning point is always possible.

God isn't punishing me, He's redirecting me. He doesn't "fix" me instantly; He walks beside me as I rebuild, step by step.

I choose to trust Him again, to treat hospital staff with kindness, and to return to Madrid, not to resume life, but to start anew.

Leaving The Priory, sunlight warms my face. No fireworks, just a quiet certainty, life isn't over. Madrid awaits, and so is the woman I'm becoming.

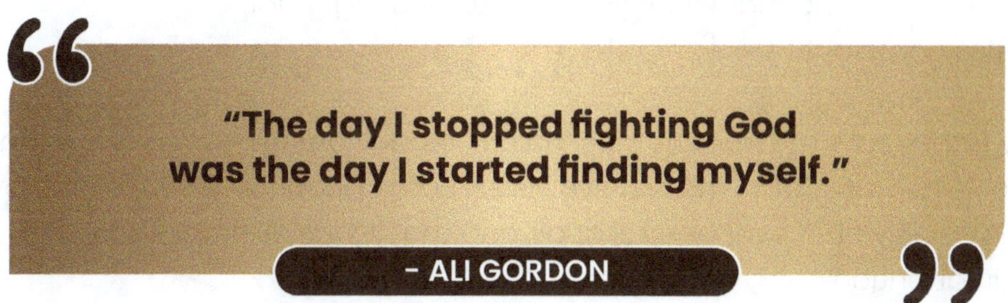

Success in Disguise

I'd love to tell you that from this day forward, everything goes smoothly, but it doesn't.

I make poor relationship choices again, as if to prove I can still "control" my own life. I resist letting God have total control. Inevitably, I end up back in hospital in Madrid for yet more "psych Obs" (psychiatric observations)!

But along the way, there are significant wins, milestones on my journey to becoming whole again.

Slowly, things begin to shift. I train as a Transformation Coach and a Fire walk Instructor, because I want to pay forward the breakthroughs I've had.

I launch LUXINOR Coaching and Training, and later, LUXINOR Publishing. They become my way of helping others step out of their comfort zones, just as I have.

Finally, I start to dream again! A published author; TV appearances; speaking at international conferences; and my proudest creation, **"The F.L.A.M.E.S. Rediscovery Roadmap." ™**

The Critics Arrive

Isn't it interesting that when you start something great, the critics come out?

My father calls my training trips "ridiculous." My brother reminds me that most start-ups fail in the first five years. Some people even whisper they don't believe I've ever been ill at all, and that it was all orchestrated to gain attention.

Also, as well as other people having their say, I start to notice that my own inner critic voice starts chipping in too! "Who are you to be doing this?" "They are right, listen to them!" "Just get a proper job with a regular salary!" As if I don't have enough to deal with!

It all stings, but it gives me great chances to learn and change! For example, I learned that criticism from others often says more about the critic than the one being criticised! I also learn that I can work with my inner critic to create a new conversation about who I truly am!

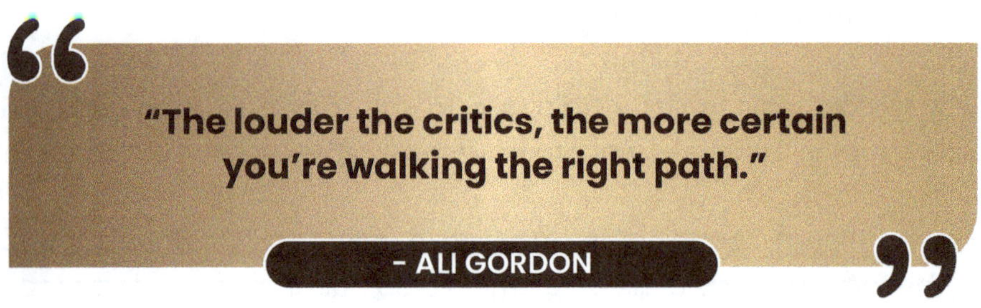

Here's the Truth

Can you relate to any of the following?...

Maybe you wake up one morning, look in the mirror, and barely recognise the person looking back.

The titles and roles that once defined you: parent, partner, professional, have faded or shifted. Without them, it's easy to feel invisible. When you stop recognising you, it chips away at your confidence and makes you question whether you still matter.

Or perhaps you've lost that sense of why. The goals that once got you out of bed don't fit anymore, and the old routines feel like wearing someone else's shoes, uncomfortable and awkward. Without purpose, the days can start to blend into one another, leaving you feeling restless and uncertain.

Or possibly even the things that should bring joy start to feel muted. You smile politely at good news, but inside it doesn't quite land. Life starts to feel more like surviving than truly living. So, wouldn't you rather be experiencing any, or even better, all, of the following instead?

Imagine waking up and feeling an unshakable sense of "This is who I am!" You see yourself with fresh eyes – strong, valuable, and deeply worthy, and you carry yourself with a quiet pride that others can't help but notice. Every choice you make comes from a place of self-respect, and it feels good... really good... to finally stand in your own truth again.

Now picture opening your eyes each morning with a burst of excitement in your chest, knowing exactly what you're moving towards. You have a reason to leap out of bed, something that lights you up from the inside out. Every day feels like a step towards a vision that matters to you, and you go to bed each night with a smile, knowing you've lived on purpose.

Finally, envision feeling that fizz of happiness in your chest again, like bubbles rising in a glass. You wake up curious about what the day will bring, and you find yourself laughing more, noticing beauty in small things, and embracing opportunities without hesitation. Life feels rich, colourful, and deliciously worth living, and the best part is, you know the joy is here to stay.

Changemakers

"OK, but how do I move from the pain to the joy of life?" I hear you asking!

Well, I believe you can achieve this by reclaiming your identity, rediscovering your purpose, and reigniting your joy.

So, what do I mean by this?

Reclaim Your Identity: Let go of old labels and roles. Remember who you are at your core and stand tall in it.

Rediscover Your Purpose: Find what matters to you now. Create fresh goals that light you up.

Reignite Your Joy: Bring back your spark. Notice the little things, say yes to new experiences, and let happiness flow again.

"The F.L.A.M.E.S. Rediscovery Roadmap."™

With your permission, I would love to share a little on how **"The F.L.A.M.E.S. Rediscovery Roadmap."™** can help you achieve reclaimed identity, rediscovered purpose, and reignited joy!

"The F.L.A.M.E.S. Rediscovery Roadmap."™ is a 6-month online group coaching program specifically designed for people aged 55 to 75 who are ready to rise again after "later-life" challenges.

It's your chance to reconnect with your true self, rebuild confidence, and find fresh purpose. A space to dust yourself off, stand tall, and set out on life's next chapter, no matter your age, no matter where you're starting from.

Each module focuses on a different area of knowledge, skills, and actions to take.

These are shown below!

FOUNDATIONS:

We start gently, no rush, no pressure. This is your space, a place where you can breathe, exhale, and reconnect with you. Not the roles you've had to play, not the titles you've carried, not the expectations that have been placed on your shoulders, but the real you.

We'll look at your skills, your strengths, and the parts of yourself that may have been tucked away under years of labels, responsibilities, and "shoulds." It's like opening a forgotten drawer and finding treasures you didn't realise you still owned, abilities you'd written off, talents you didn't know you still had, sparks of curiosity and creativity that are ready to be brought back to life. Together, we'll gently peel those layers back, letting you stand in your own name again, confident, grounded, and clear about who you are and what you bring to the table. This is where the groundwork is laid, the solid foundation that will support everything that comes next on your journey.

LIBERTY:

Once you've got your footing, it's time to loosen the grip of those invisible chains, the limitations that have been holding you back for far too long. In the **LIBERTY** module, we gently but deliberately start dismantling the old stories you've been told (and maybe even told yourself) about what you can and cannot do.

You'll begin to recognise the fears that have been quietly steering your choices, the ones that whisper, "you're too old," "you're not ready," or "it's too risky." Instead of letting those voices control the narrative, you'll learn how to face them, challenge them, and release them. This isn't about pretending those fears never existed, it's about taking away their power. It's about giving yourself permission to dream without boundaries, to imagine a life that feels lighter, freer, and more you than it has in years.

ADVENTURE:

This is the stage where we throw open the doors to possibility and let fresh air flood in. This is where you step beyond the familiar and give yourself permission to explore, to play, and to say "yes" to things that stir your curiosity. Maybe it's trying a creative pursuit you've always admired from a distance, learning a skill that feels delightfully outside your comfort zone, travelling somewhere new, or even pursuing a passion you'd quietly buried under years of "maybe someday."

It's not about reckless leaps, it's about thoughtful, courageous steps that awaken parts of you that have been sleeping. In this module, you start to rediscover that spark inside, the one that still craves excitement, growth, and joy, and you learn how to nurture it, so it becomes part of your everyday life.

MASTERY:

The **MASTERY** module is where confidence really starts to grow. You'll be learning and developing new skills, not just because it's good for you, but because it makes life richer, more independent, and a lot more fun.

You'll take on challenges that once felt intimidating and turn them into small, satisfying wins. Whether it's conquering a bit of tech, picking up a creative talent, or deepening your knowledge in something you love, this module proves to you that you're still growing, still capable, and still able to surprise yourself, and that's a great feeling.

ENGAGEMENT:

The **ENGAGEMENT** module is where you start weaving this new energy, freedom, and curiosity into everyday life. You begin showing up for the things, and the people, that matter to you.

It could mean joining a local group, volunteering for a cause close to your heart, or simply connecting more deeply with the friends and family you already have. **ENGAGEMENT** says, "I'm here, I'm involved, and I'm part of something bigger than me." It's about building a life that feels connected, purposeful, and satisfying, on your own terms.

SUPPORT:

This is where you establish your safety net, and your Elite F1 Pit Crew rolled into one. This is where you connect with people who understand you, who believe in you, and are there to remind you why you started, even on the tough days. It's about having a circle that celebrates your wins, lifts you when you stumble, and walks beside you every step of the way. **SUPPORT** turns this from a lonely climb into a shared adventure. Let's face it, life is just better when you've got the right people in your corner!

Each Module also has its own Programme Title, see below!

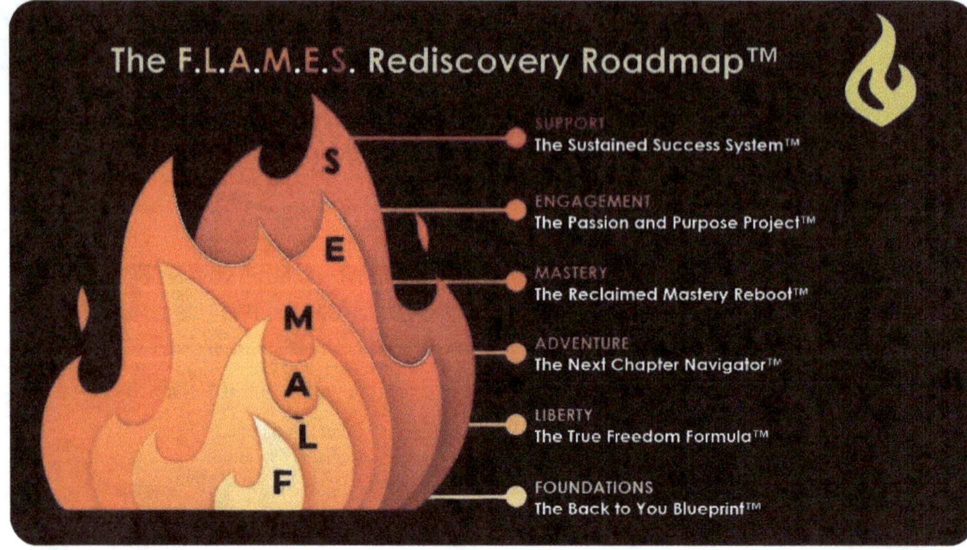

For example, **FOUNDATIONS** is ***"The Back to You Blueprint"***™

I would love to introduce this programme in a little more depth. Here we cover FOUR themes:

FOCUS – *Make space for you.* Shift your attention inward. Put life on mute, silence the to-do lists, roles and expectations, so you can tune into yourself. Using techniques such as Introductions to: "Ideal Average Day" visualisation, mindfulness exercises, and breathing exercises. 

Pause. Breathe. Begin again.

FIND – *Rediscover hidden treasures.* Dig beneath the layers to uncover forgotten strengths, talents and sparks of curiosity waiting to come alive again. Using techniques such as Introductions to: childhood strengths and talents exercise, and comparison with today's identified strengths and talents. 

Uncover the gold within.

FREE – *Release what isn't really you.* Let go of the "shoulds" and old expectations that weigh you down, creating space for authenticity. Using techniques such as Introductions to: inner voices, identification, reframing from "should" to "get to".

Let go! Feel lighter!

FIRM – *Stand strong in your own name.* Root yourself in clarity and confidence. Stand tall, grounded in who you are and what you bring. Using techniques such as Introductions to: the concept of our true core self, the "Who am I?" exercise.

Rooted. Ready. Rocking it!

Each of the other Programmes follow a similar structure, with its own relevant sub steps to follow.

Here's why this course is unique!

What makes **The F.L.A.M.E.S. Rediscovery Roadmap™** stand out is that we don't just throw piles of information at you. Most people finish a course with a notebook full of half-scribbled ideas that get tucked away and forgotten.

Sound familiar? I've done it too!

With LUXINOR Coaching and Training, change happens differently. You're given time to absorb what you learn, reflect on how it fits your life, and most importantly, put it into action.

Throughout **"The F.L.A.M.E.S. Rediscovery Roadmap"** ™, information, reflection, and application are woven together, so transformation isn't just a hope at the end, it's happening every step of the way.

> **"Reclaiming your life isn't about going back –
> it's about moving forward with purpose.**
>
> **– ALI GORDON**

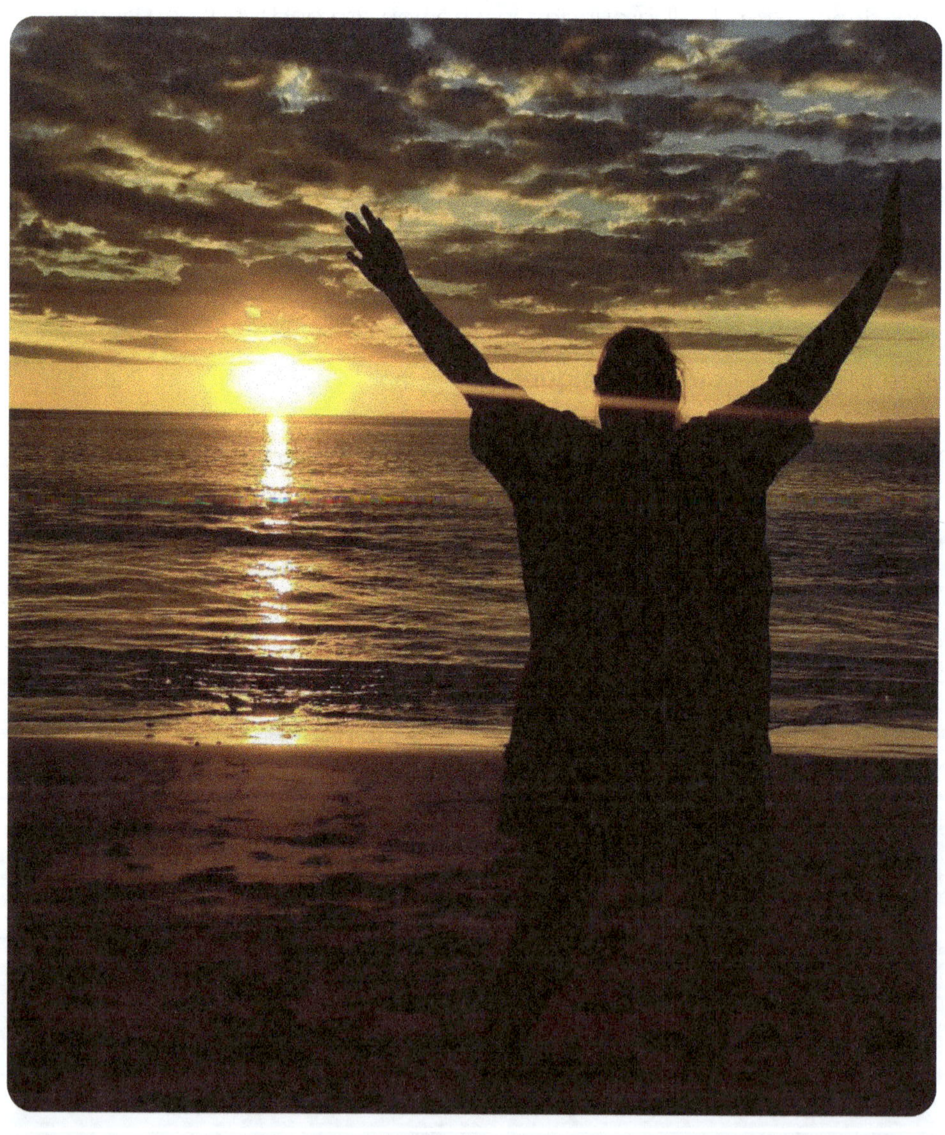

So, to Wrap Up…

If having read this chapter you resonate with anything I have said, you can see how this programme might help you move from the pains you are experiencing to your dream life, or you can hear the words on these pages calling to you, then I encourage you to get in touch to have an **"Ignite The Fire"** chat with me in person. Here we can get to know each other better. You can also find out more about what's needed to change your life from hurting to healing and how **"The F.L.A.M.E.S. Rediscovery Roadmap."™** can help you with this.

I hit 60 this year. I've been "sectioned", broken, misunderstood, and written off because of my age and emotion regulation issues more times than I care to mention…

…but I am here - and so are you!

Remember: it's never too late for being great! If I can rise from my lowest point in a locked ward to creating a life filled with purpose, joy, and impact… then you can too!

All it takes is that first, trembling step; and I'll walk it with you!

Ali Gordon is a Transformation Coach and Fire walk Instructor who empowers people aged 55 –75 to rediscover their identity, purpose, and joy no matter what life throws their way.

Her book, **"Hope in the Darkness: One Heart's Journey to Becoming Whole"**, charts the messy, miraculous path from breakdown to breakthrough, with a few divine nudges and guinea pig cuddle breaks along the way.

Based in Madrid with her four furry flatmates and an overly generous fridge, she now passionately shares her life journey to inspire others that they too can create fulfilling, exciting, and joy-filled lives.

Discover more at: **www.luxinorcoachingandtraining.com.**

Take that first step now!

Scan the QR code to sign up for an "Ignite the Fire" chat so you can start writing the next chapter of your life with energy, purpose, and joy!

"Your next chapter starts right here!"

– ALI GORDON

CHAPTER 3
CRACKED BUT NOT BROKEN

AN ORTHOPAEDIC SURGEON'S JOURNEY FROM INJURY TO INSIGHT

"*Pain was my teacher, silence my challenge, and advocacy my mission - together they became the fire that shaped my voice.*"

– *George Zarifopoulos*

...

We all carry cracks.

Some are in the bones we've pushed too far. Others are in the trust we've given to systems that promised to protect us. Most are invisible, hairline fractures in the spirit, hidden behind professional smiles and steady hands.

This is my journey, from the surgeon's table to the patient's bed, from physical collapse to professional redemption. Along the way, I meet the forgotten workers whose stories are rarely told, and the rare managers who dare to listen. This work is for them. For us. For everyone caught between the grind of duty and the weight of pain. Back pain doesn't clock out when your shift ends. It follows you like a shadow, creeping into your most intimate spaces. It interrupts your sleep, dulls your concentration, dampens your joy. It chips away at the foundation of your identity.

It doesn't matter whether you're lifting, driving, sitting, or standing for hours, the toll isn't just physical. It grinds down the spirit. Before the injury, my life was a rhythm of theatre lights, scalpel handles, and the quiet hum of suction machines. The smell of antiseptic was as familiar as my morning coffee, and the weight of surgical gloves felt like a second skin. Most people imagine surgery as constant adrenaline, but in truth, it's equal parts focus and patience. There are stretches where you're as still as a statue, your back inclined at an awkward angle, your neck bent just so, while you work through layers of muscle and bone. The operating table becomes your universe, everything beyond its sterile perimeter fades into irrelevance. I thrived in it. The quiet concentration broken only by the steady beep of monitors. The unspoken choreography between scrub nurse and surgeon, where a raised eyebrow meant "suture" and a slight nod indicated "retractor." There was a pride in knowing that for those hours, someone's life was literally in my hands, and that I could change their tomorrow with precision and care. In those days, I was invincible. Or so I believed.

Changemakers

My typical day began at 7:30 AM with rounds, checking on post-operative patients before the hospital stirred to full life. By 9.00 AM, I was scrubbing in for the first case. The ritual was like meditation as arms are raised, water cascading from elbows, the methodical cleansing that separated the ordinary world from the sacred space of surgery.

Between cases, I'd grab coffee from the machine that perpetually needed repair, its motor grinding like an old man's joints.
The orthopaedic department was a tight community, we shared gallows humour about difficult cases, celebrated successful outcomes with quiet satisfaction, and carried each other through the inevitable losses that came with our profession. There's a saying in surgery: "Your body will remember before your mind does." The hours of standing, twisting, and lifting leave their mark like sediment in a riverbed. We all joked about our sore backs after a twelve-hour shift, comparing ourselves to the rugby players we'd patched up, warriors bearing honourable scars. But deep down, we thought we were indestructible.

After all, we were the ones who fixed broken bones, not the ones who broke them.

But there is this paradox; we treat people who are in pain with more pain.

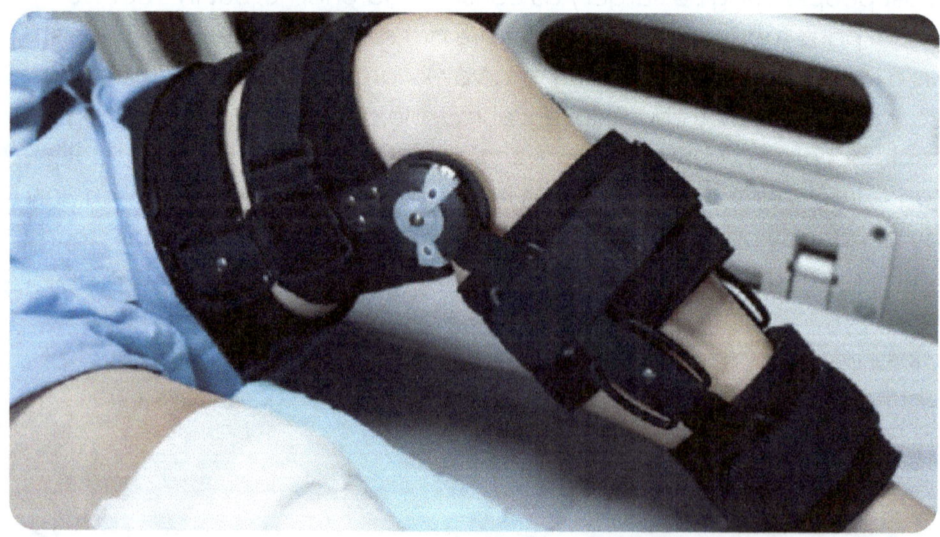

But here's the truth most don't hear, back pain is not always a life sentence. It's a signal. A challenge. And with the right knowledge, small daily adjustments, and a commitment to change, it can be managed, softened, and often reversed.

What follows is more than a memoir. It's part personal account, part practical manual, and part cultural critique. It's about the science of back pain, yes, but it's also about the human cost of neglect, when people are left to fight their battles alone.

It begins just after Christmas, twenty-five winters ago. The air is sharp enough to sting the lungs; daylight fades by mid-afternoon. I'm in the hospital's administrative wing. The waiting room is stark, metal filing cabinets, dull faux-leather chairs, faded posters promising better health systems. The air smells faintly of ink and bureaucracy.

The receptionist looks up. "You can sit, Mr. Zee."

I shake my head. "Standing hurts less."

The intercom crackles: "Send George in."

The hospital manager sits behind a desk large enough to stage an operation. Shoulders like a retired rugby player, face grey, eyes like granite, mouth rarely bent into a smile.

Without looking up: "Well, George, what's the matter?"

I steady myself, my spine protesting every breath. "Six months ago, in theatre, we were repositioning a massive patient. The timing failed. The others dropped away. I took the full weight. Something cracked. I finished the surgery, but I left the theatre in pain, and it's never stopped. I've only been given painkillers. If I go on sick leave the Department will suffer, and you know it. I need physiotherapy.
Please send me to Occupational health."

He raises a hand. "First, don't blackmail me by saying the Department won't function without you. Second, your doctor says it's muscular. Refer yourself to physio."

"I can't. Regulations won't allow it."

He picks up his pen. He is not even looking at me. "You can go now. I'm busy."

Dismissed.

I walk out hollow; my plea dissolved into the walls. Something in my spine had cracked that day in theatre, but it's my faith in the system that feels broken. Six months pass. The pain becomes constant, less a sharp cry, more a dull companion. My body curves into new shapes. My stride shortens. My moods changed. At the dinner table I am absent. In bed I growl like a wounded animal. Nobody wants to be around me. My family feels the shift, my children tread lightly, my wife grows quiet, even the dog greets me with a cautious wag.

I stop looking in mirrors. I stop asking for help. Like a fractured bone left unattended, I begin to set wrong.

Until one August afternoon, walking toward the canteen, drawn by the smell of roast beef, I hear behind me: "George?"

Turn like a log. The spine is not following what the brain is telling it to do. It's Mike, an old friend, now a metabolic physician.
"You've vanished," he says.

I shrug. "Back pain. No one's helping. I'm surviving."

He studies me for a moment. "Come to my clinic. Now. Before lunch."

Two days later: "Borderline diabetic. Hypertension's starting. You need a total change, or medication for life."

Something in me snaps again, but this time it's not defeat, it's defiance. "Me? Pills for life? I'm a doctor. I prescribe them, I don't take them." That was my line in the sand.

The next six months are my proving ground.
Recovery isn't cinematic. It's not a quick montage. It's awkward, slow, and often lonely. I walk, first to the end of the street, then around the block, then miles. I read everything: pain science, posture mechanics, metabolic health. I rebuild not just my body, but my understanding.

Slowly, stiffness loosens. My blood pressure settles. My energy returns. My family smiles more. At work, I lose the nickname "Papa Smurf" for my hunched, blue-scrubbed frame.

The crack in my body is healing. The crack in my confidence begins to knit too.
Then a nurse comes into my clinic. She lifts patients daily, smiles through every shift—but pops painkillers in the break room. Nobody asks. Nobody notices. Until she ends up in surgery herself.

Her story mirrors mine. And I realise, there are thousands like us. Drivers. Nurses. Warehouse staff. All enduring quietly. All underserved.

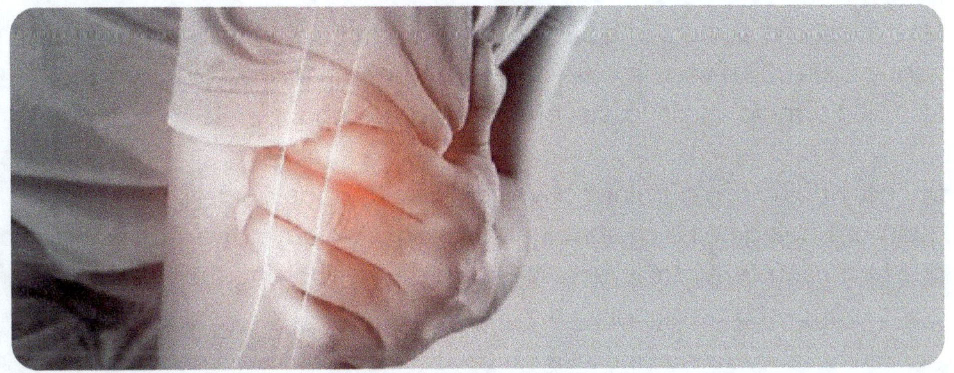

So, I built something: The **E.R.A.S.E.** Low Back Pain Formula.

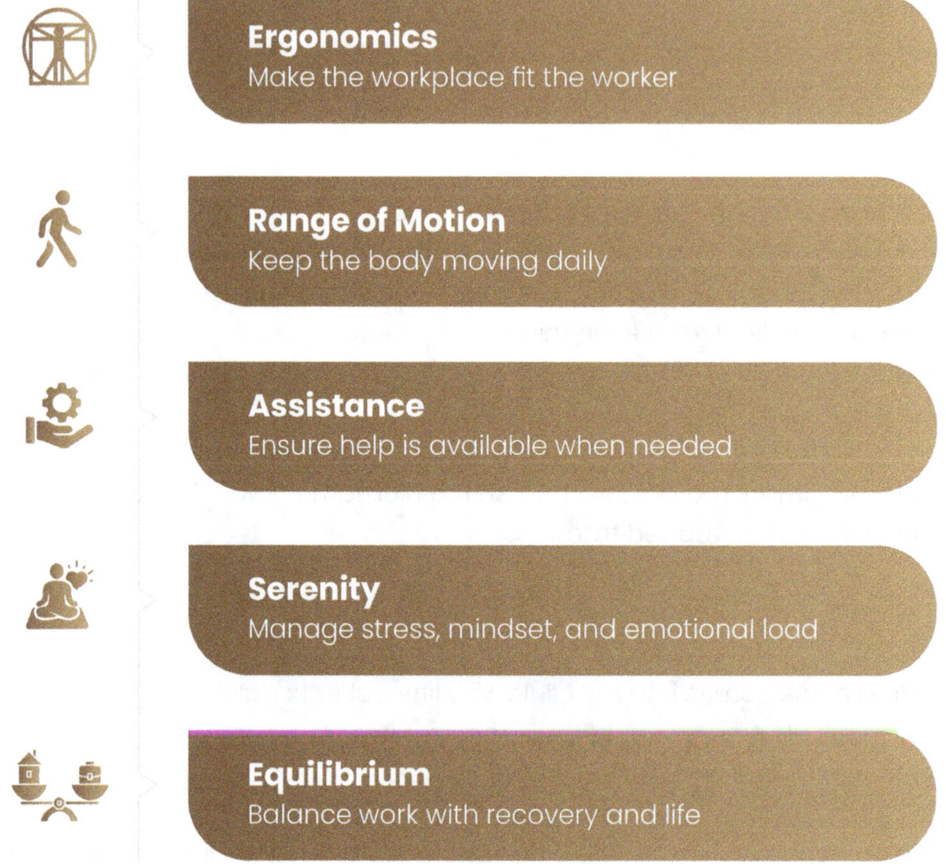

It's not theory - it's lived. Tested. Proven.

Mike and Sara, owners of a 25-driver transport company, were losing nearly £200,000 a year in costs related to back pain. They applied the E.R.A.S.E. Formula, those losses almost disappeared.

Donna, who ran an administrative services company, was haemorrhaging half a million annually from sick leave and staff turnover due to musculoskeletal issues. Within a year of applying the formula, her costs dropped dramatically.

These aren't abstract successes; they are proof that cracks can be repaired when the right care and attention are applied.

My spine cracked. But I was not broken. Pain became my teacher. Silence became my challenge. Advocacy became my mission.

If you're a leader, this work will give you tools to protect your people, and your bottom line. If you're a worker, it will give you strategies to reclaim your body and your life. Recovery isn't about "getting back to where you were." It's about moving forward with wisdom you didn't have before.

Because sometimes, a crack doesn't mean collapse.
Sometimes, it's where the light gets in.

Even in pain, there is strength.
Even in silence, there is a voice.
Even in the hardest moments, there is hope.

We all carry cracks. But cracked is not broken.

And the very place where you think you've fractured, might be the place you begin again.

Let's begin. Let's walk this road together.

But let's approach one of the subjects and answer the question,
Why Movement Matters?

Let's begin with it.

Do people move when they are in pain? The answer is, NO. Because when pain arrives, the first instinct is stillness. Even the breath is stopped. We freeze. We guard. We avoid. We stay in bed, skip the gym, decline invitations, stop walking the dog. It's natural. Pain sends a primal warning: *stay still or you'll make it worse.*

But for back pain, especially mechanical back pain - this message is misleading. Prolonged immobility doesn't heal. It hurts.

The spine, like all joints, is designed to move. Motion nourishes the discs, lubricates the joints, strengthens the supporting muscles, and signals to the brain that the body is safe. When we don't move, we stiffen. We weaken. We become more sensitive to pain, not less.

The phrase "motion is lotion" isn't just a cliché, it's neurobiology. Regular, varied movement reduces the threat signals the brain interprets as pain. Movement improves circulation, encourages lymphatic drainage, and provides your intervertebral discs with the fluid exchange they require to remain healthy. Without movement, those sponge-like discs become brittle. The muscles that support your spine begin to atrophy.
The fascia stiffens.

And it's not only the musculoskeletal system that benefits, but movement also directly influences the body's hormonal system. Every step, every stretch, every rotation sets off a cascade of biochemical signals. Exercise increases the production of endorphins, natural painkillers that elevate mood and dull discomfort. It reduces cortisol, the stress hormone that, when elevated chronically, contributes to inflammation and sensitises the nervous system to pain. Gentle movement increases levels of dopamine and serotonin, two neurotransmitters associated with motivation, focus, and emotional regulation.

Perhaps most striking is the effect on insulin sensitivity. Physical activity enhances the muscles' ability to uptake glucose without insulin, thereby reducing blood sugar levels and improving metabolic flexibility. For individuals who like I was, are teetering on the edge of type 2 diabetes, this is more than a bonus. It's a lifeline.

When you move, you're not just stretching a joint. You're activating an entire endocrine orchestra: lowering blood pressure, balancing hormones, and promoting an internal chemistry that supports healing.

I saw this in myself. I see it in my patients. And the research agrees. Clinical guidelines from the National Institute for Health and Care Excellence (NICE) recommend staying active as one of the most effective treatments for non-specific low back pain. A landmark study published in The Lancet reinforced the evidence that bed rest delays recovery, while movement accelerates it.

Yet, culturally, we resist this truth. Patients are often told by well-meaning friends or even outdated practitioners to rest. To lie flat. To "take it easy." But for how long? And at what cost?

This doesn't mean reckless movement. It doesn't mean ignoring pain or pushing through red flags. It means the kind of intentional, progressive movement that meets your body where it is and nudges it, gently, forward. During my own recovery, I started with ten steps. That's all I could manage. But those ten became twenty. Twenty became a stroll. A stroll became a brisk walk. Each day, I wrote it down. I tracked not just distance, but how I felt. Was my posture better? Was my breathing deeper? Did I feel more human?

Because pain does something strange to time. It shrinks your world. You measure life by minutes, until the next dose of painkillers, until the next spasm. Movement, done wisely, starts to widen that world again. I learned to carry resistance bands in my coat pocket. I stretched against lampposts. I practiced hip rolls at traffic lights. Movement wasn't a gym appointment. It was survival.

I shared this with my patients. I told them how the shock absorbers of their body are faulty and how to activate the additional ones. Drivers were delighted with the explanation as this was so easy for them to understand. They were laughing, asking me what brand of shock absorbers they need to buy from the store. One elderly man, a retired lorry driver, began setting an alarm to stand every hour. He'd walk around the garden, regardless of weather. After six weeks, his back pain eased. His blood pressure dropped. His smile returned.

Changemakers

Another patient, a midwife, started incorporating micro-breaks between appointments. Ten squats. A shoulder roll. Deep diaphragmatic breathing. Her headaches diminished. Her back spasms stopped.

Mike and Sara's drivers added a 3-minute movement sequence at every delivery stop: spinal rotations, leg swings, shoulder shrugs. At first, they laughed. It felt silly. They were teasing each other for the peculiar movements they were doing. They felt that they were part of a choreography. They thought that they were in Broadway. But the attitude changed. Within weeks, the laughter was joined by relief. They were competing. They were comparing their "positions" and their techniques. Younger drivers were instructing some older and the camaraderie and networking grew stronger. By month three, their health records had changed.

Movement reclaims what pain tries to steal. Motion is fun.

It gives you agency. It gives you rhythm. It gives you choice. But perhaps most powerfully, it restores trust.

Because chronic pain erodes trust in the body. You feel betrayed by the very frame you live in. Movement, approached with kindness and consistency, helps repair that relationship. It says: "I can move, and nothing terrible happens." It rebuilds the broken contract between body and brain.

So, here's what I offer, not as a prescription, but as a promise:

Move every hour, even if just to change position.

Walk outside daily, no matter how short the distance.

Reintroduce safe spinal motion, side bends, rotations, pelvic tilts.

This is not about reclaiming youth or chasing athleticism. No one is asking you to become a marathon runner or a vault jumper. It's about regaining belonging in your body. It's about walking back into your life, step by step.

Because recovery doesn't always roar. Sometimes, it whispers, "Move." And when you listen - your body remembers.

Let's keep going.

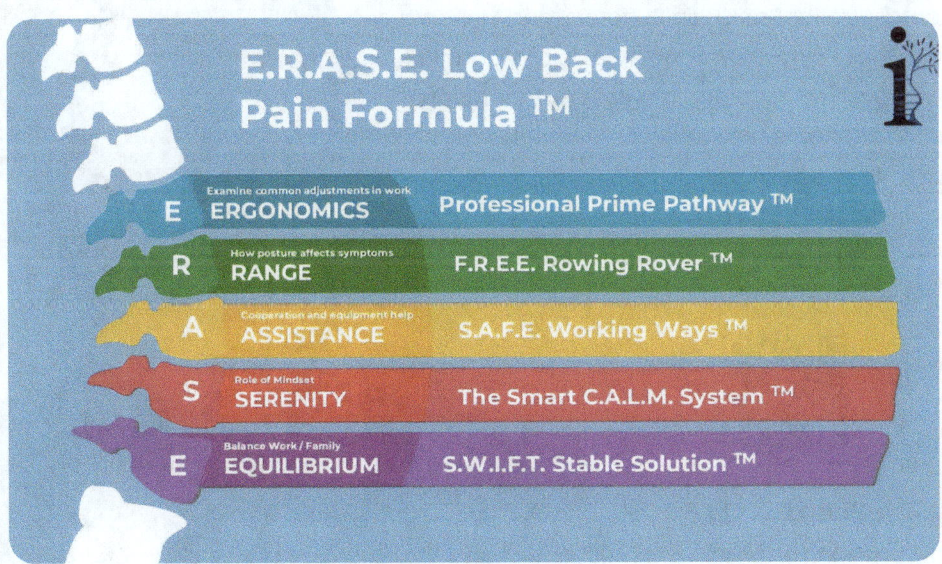

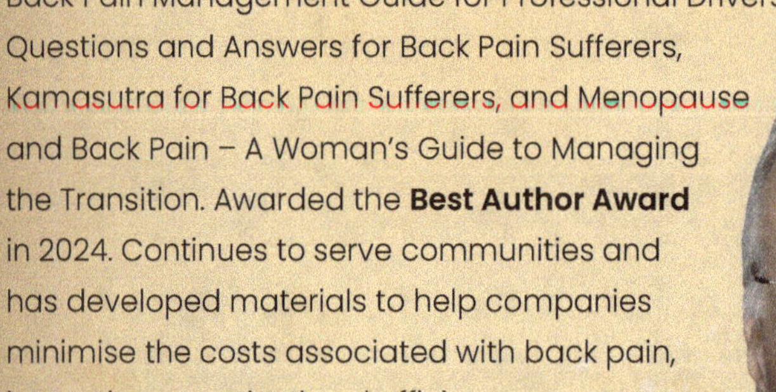

George Zafiropolous is a Senior Consultant Orthopaedic Surgeon, Researcher, Author and Educator. Trained in the EU, UK, and USA. Awarded a scholarship by the British Orthopaedic Association. Conducted research on the biomechanics of the musculoskeletal system, leading to further training at the Hospital for Special Surgery, New York and Mayo Clinic, Rochester, USA. Visiting Lecturer (University in Greece), where he established a course on the Biomechanics of the Musculoskeletal System. University Lecturer and Visiting Professor in United Kingdom. Led Orthopaedic Department with strong skills in management, organisation, and communication, committed to achieving goals. Member of several national and international Scientific Societies and Speaker at numerous scientific conferences. Author of scientific books, including Healthcare Heroes: A Comprehensive Guide for Future Health Professionals and Functional Anatomy and Basic Biomechanics for the Musculoskeletal System, and multiple peer-reviewed articles published in scientific journals. In recent years, following personal experience, committed to in-depth research on chronic low back pain management and the holistic impact of symptoms on individuals and their environment—particularly in corporations. Member of Professional Speakers Academy. Author of series of books on low back pain management, including Pain Management for Chronic Back Pain Sufferers, From Back Pain to Productivity, Back Pain Management Guide for Professional Drivers, Questions and Answers for Back Pain Sufferers, Kamasutra for Back Pain Sufferers, and Menopause and Back Pain – A Woman's Guide to Managing the Transition. Awarded the **Best Author Award** in 2024. Continues to serve communities and has developed materials to help companies minimise the costs associated with back pain, improving organisational efficiency.

Scan the QR code for More!

CHAPTER 4
BREAKING BEYOND YOUR BARRIERS

"Living life to your full
potential means living
life on YOUR terms."

- Colleen Stevenson

Have you ever carried a secret so deep it feels sewn into your skin? Not just hidden in your mind but woven through your bones. You've built a life around keeping it contained with years of silence, shame, and survival. On the outside, you look fine. You smile in photos. You laugh at the right times. You keep going. Maybe people even envy you, thinking you've "got it together."

But inside, it's like you're moving through water, everything heavy, muffled, slow.

The truth is, it's not always the event itself that hurts the most. It's the weight of keeping it locked away, unspoken and unresolved. The longer you carry it, the heavier it gets, until your body feels like it's holding its breath all the time.

You find ways to cope, wine that warms you just enough to dull the edges, food that comforts for a moment, endless scrolling, shopping, keeping yourself so busy you don't have to feel a thing. You tell yourself "This is just life."

But deep down, you know it's not. You can feel it in the knot in your stomach, the tightness in your chest, the way your shoulders never quite relax.

Pain that sits in the body too long doesn't just stay pain - it becomes tension, exhaustion. And if left there, it can turn into something far more dangerous. Dis-ease becomes disease.

I'm not here to "fix" you. I'm here to tell you your story matters. Your secret deserves to be heard. And healing is possible.

I know - because I've lived it.

It's September 1993. I'm eleven-years-old, standing barefoot at the top of a staircase. The house is quiet, but it's the wrong kind of quiet - the kind that makes you strain to hear what's coming.

Changemakers

Behind me, my bedroom door is closed, though I know a flimsy door isn't much of a barrier. To my left, a small window looks out onto a street washed in sunlight, but in here the air feels stale.

The carpet beneath my toes is stained, crawling with fleas. The walls are patched with damp. My stomach is twisting, because downstairs, I hear it – the sound of a key turning in the lock.

The smell comes first, before he even steps inside: that sharp, sickly-sweet Joop aftershave. It hits me like a warning.

Then I see him – greasy brown hair hanging over his forehead, gap between his teeth, ears that stick out like they're tuned to my fear. He doesn't have to say a word. My pulse is already hammering. My hands tremble so hard I clasp them together just to hide it.

I feel the weight of everything that's already happened pressing down on my chest. And then, something inside me snaps.

"DON'T YOU EVER TOUCH ME AGAIN!" The words tear out of my throat before I can second-guess them. "IF YOU DO, I'LL CALL THE POLICE!"

The silence after is louder than the shout. His face hardens, but he doesn't move. My heart feels like it's going to burst. Part of me wants to run past him and out the door, but my feet are frozen.

In my head, the thoughts come fast: What if he comes upstairs? What if he hurts me again? But then another voice cuts through: Not this time. Not now.

I think about telling my mum, but I picture her – slumped in her chair, drink in hand, eyes glazed. She wouldn't hear me. And even if she did, she'd twist it into something that fits her version of reality. I think about a teacher. Maybe they'd listen. But what if they told the police? What if they took me away from everything I know – even the bad parts?

The fear of losing my fragile stability outweighs the fear of staying silent.

So, I make the choice: I tell no one. Not Mum. Not Dad. Not a friend. I wrap my shame around me like a blanket and bury the truth deep inside, where I think no one will find it.

But burying a secret doesn't kill it. It just grows roots.

My older brother didn't just take my innocence - he locked away the girl I was meant to be. I was like a bird with wings made for the sky, trapped behind bars. I didn't just hide the memories. I hid me.

As the years passed, I tried so many things to break free....therapists, counsellors, and yes there was an element of this that served me - So much so that I became a mum to two beautiful girls and for a moment, I hoped their love will heal me... But motherhood doesn't erase pain...

Nothing seemed to help me move forward. In those years I had one loyal companion, my dear friend Oyster Bay, New Zealand's finest white wine, and then one day, life throws me something I didn't see coming.

Changemakers

It's November 18th, 2014. The hospital waiting room is full of glowing, pregnant women. I feel out of place among their laughter and round bellies. The smell of disinfectant is sharp in my nose and the phone at the front desk rings endlessly.

Dr. Andrew Prentice steps out - a short man, greying hair, warm smile behind thick glasses. "Hi, Colleen. Take a seat. I wasn't expecting to see you today."

"Oh? I thought we had a follow-up. You removed the polyps from my womb, remember?"

"Yes, I remember… but your notes are with the oncology team. You have been informed of that?"

"The oncology team? No… what's that?"

He pauses, and my stomach drops before he even speaks. "Colleen… the results show you have cancer of the womb."

The words float in the air, and I wait for them to land, to make sense.

They don't. "You must have made a mistake. I'm thirty-three. I'm here for a check-up. Cancer? No. Not me."

But the look in his eyes tells me there's no mistake.

For two weeks, I don't leave my bed. I cry. I rage. I ask the universe, "Why me? Haven't I been through enough?" I replay my life like a film I wish I could rewrite.

Then, one morning, my eight-year-old daughter Jaz stands in the doorway, ready for school. Her dad waits outside. She looks at me, her small face serious, and asks, "Mummy… are you going to die?"

Something in me shifts. "No, darling," I say, pulling her into my arms. "I'm not going anywhere."

After she leaves, I face the bathroom mirror. My reflection is pale and tired, yet beneath the weariness, a faint flicker still remains.

You've survived worse, I tell myself. If you can live through the pain of your past, you can live through this. Those girls need you.

No one will open this cage for you, Colleen—you have to unlock it yourself.

The road back isn't easy. People I thought would support me vanish. Some mock me "You're boring now, why aren't you drinking?" Others make jokes "Are you a rabbit? All you eat is greens!" Their words sting, but they don't break me.

I keep going. I read every self-development book I can get my hands on: The Secret, The Monk Who Sold His Ferrari, Feel the Fear and Do It

Anyway. But reading isn't enough. I find a coach who teaches me how to go deeper - to face the parts of me I've avoided my whole life.

I meet my inner child. I listen to her. I tell her she matters. Slowly, the bars around my cage begin to bend. I forgive my brother - not because what he did was okay, but because I refuse to carry the poison any longer. Forgiveness becomes freedom.

That freedom lights a fire in me. I train as a coach. I start helping women unlock their own cages. And now ten years cancer-free, I love nothing more than knowing that I've guided hundreds of women into living life to the fullest.

That's why I created my **Break Beyond Your Barriers Blueprint™** - to help women reconnect with who they truly are, so they can stop surviving and start living.

One of them is Emily. When she came to me, she was convinced she wasn't "good enough" for a promotion she wanted. We traced that belief back to a single comment from a teacher when she was eleven. We reframed the story, gave her the tools to rewrite it. She applied for the job - and got it. Now she leads a team of ten.

How did she do it? By shifting her mindset. Your mindset is the lens through which you see and experience the world. It influences your thoughts, emotions, actions and ultimately shapes your reality. But the first step to shifting your mindset is AWARENESS!

The aim of AWARENESS is to gain clarity on our reactive behaviours and patterns which are rooted in the beliefs we hold. Our beliefs come from our past conditioning and life experiences...and what if there are conscious patterns or behaviours that feel normal to us but at the same time (without realising) limit us?

NOW WHY IS THAT IMPORTANT TO UNDERSTAND?

Well, without the awareness of your reactive behaviours and patterns, you will be limited from the life that you deserve. You limit yourself from your potential successes and stop yourself from pursuing your goals.

For instance, a long time ago, I believed that money was the root of all evil (which wasn't my own belief in the first place, but I'll explain that in a moment) but because that belief was so deeply rooted, the moment I received money was the moment I'd let go of it. I'd either spend it recklessly , gift it away etc, and I had no savings because a part of me truly believed that if I have money then people would see me as selfish or greedy, particularly my Dad, because he was the one that used to say it aloud when I was a little girl. It was never my belief to have and hold onto...and you know what maybe it wasn't my dad's either, maybe it was just a family loyalty passed down in ancestry.

And I wonder how many others are out there with the same unconscious belief, spending money recklessly on unnecessary things rather than investing it into what really matters and using it to help them achieve their goals.

And once I realised I had no AWARENESS of what I was doing (unconsciously), I soon changed the narrative.

"Until you make the unconscious conscious it will rule your life, and you will continue to call it fate" - Carl Jung

A common mistake I see is people confuse awareness with action, because whilst awareness is essential, it's only the first step, and some people think that once they have the understanding about themselves, things will automatically change for them.

But here's the thing, without looking inward, without taking an honest look at ourselves, without looking under the carpet at what dust, junk and shit is hiding there, it's only going to get worse, because you may potentially trip over it causing more damage, or it might be harder for you to clean up in the long run.

How do I know this? Because it happened to me. I refused to look under that carpet. Why didn't I? Because it felt scary at the time, I didn't want to think about re-living the sexual abuse I'd endured in childhood, it was the unknown, but guess what? My lack of self-awareness was holding me back from a whole load of unknown opportunities. Unknown opportunities that have created a better life for me!

So, I knew that when Emily came to me after her free clarity call, I had to share the 3 C's of self-awareness with her.

CLARIFY

Emily clarified every self-limiting belief she had about herself (i.e. I'm not good enough).

CONSIDER

Emily considered where the self-limiting beliefs came from, (i.e. Past Experience or Past Conditioning).

CONSEQUENCE

Emily looked at what had been the consequences of having this limiting belief.

Once Emily had found the awareness, she was ready to take the next step (BIG ACTION). So, with her permission I took her through a 1:1 deep hypnotherapy session called The Time Lens Method™. The awareness became clearer, and she could gain a deeper understanding of how and why this limiting belief was holding her back. This also helped her reframe her thought process and create an empowering belief, rather than a limiting one.

So, when it comes to awareness think of it this way....

Imagine you're driving on a foggy road. At first everything is hazy, and you can barely see what's ahead, making it hard to navigate. But slowly the fog begins to lift. As it clears, the road becomes more visible and you can see the turns and obstacles ahead, making your destination much clearer.

Awareness is like a fog lifting. The clearer your awareness the easier it is to move forward with purpose, avoiding roadblocks and making confident decisions.

Living life to the fullest is a choice. I chose it. Emily chose it. And you can choose it too.

Healing isn't just about surviving the worst days; it's about creating the best ones. Every scar you carry can be the foundation for something beautiful.

Your fullest life is waiting, but it won't come knocking, you have to open the door.

So, if my story has stirred something in you, don't ignore it. That's your inner child, calling you home.

The question is - will you answer to her?

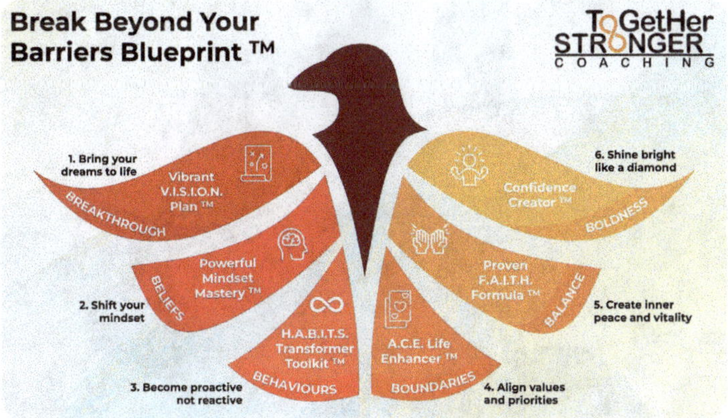

Colleen Stevenson is a Level 7 Holistic Mindset Coach, NLP Practitioner, and author who knows first-hand the power of turning pain into purpose. After surviving childhood trauma and a life-threatening cancer diagnosis, Colleen rebuilt her life from the inside out - and now helps women worldwide do the same. Through her award-winning *Break Beyond Your Barriers Blueprint™*, she empowers clients to heal, reclaim their confidence, and create a life they truly love. Colleen's mission is to show women that no matter their past, they can rise, thrive, and live life to the fullest - unapologetically and on their own terms.

Scan the QR code for More!

CHAPTER 5
THE FUTURE OF LEADERSHIP

"The future of leadership will not be measured by titles or control, but by the power to inspire, the purpose to serve, and the prosperity we create together."

– Simone Heinzelmann

When we drive a car, we're required to pass both theory and practice. Why? Because without it, accidents happen. But how much more complex is a human being? And how many accidents do we create every day? Emotional crashes, mental meltdowns, broken trust, lost clients...

My vision is that one day, the High IMPACT Leadership License will be a standard for everyone in a leading position. Until then, let me share a few short stories with you. Maybe you'll recognise yourself in one of them and become part of the movement.

There's the **snooze-button morning:** the alarm rings, but you hit snooze again. Last night was restless, and today you're dragging yourself into the office, hoping not to make that one wrong move that could cost you everything you've worked for, your position, your career, even your business.

Or the **rat-race glacier:** every step you take, the ice cracks and another crevasse open. Your to-do list multiplies like hidden crevasses under fresh snow. You help everyone else cross, but wonder, "Who's checking the rope for me?" And sometimes you catch yourself whispering, "Is this really all there is? What about my potential?"

Then there's **the promotion illusion:** you thought the summit would bring relief. Instead, the air is thinner. Yes, the title is higher, the salary larger, but so are the bills, the expectations, the lifestyle.

And finally, the **time trap,** your child asks for just one hour on a hot summer day to enjoy some ice cream together. Your partner longs to go to a weekend dance festival, which was once your shared passion. And your answer stays the same "Sorry, I don't have time." Each "no" feels like a rope you cut, and once cut, it's hard to tie back in.

If one of these stories' stings, you're not alone. **77% of senior executives report symptoms of burnout (KPMG).** The World Health Organisation even calls it a workplace syndrome. These are not weaknesses; they're

signals that to climb today's peaks; your current equipment
needs an upgrade.

But here's the good news, every expedition has a basecamp. A place
where you can regroup, pick better gear, and choose a smarter route.
That's what the **High IMPACT Leadership License** is: a rope system, a
high-tech GPS, a set of human technologies that allow you to climb
higher, without burning out.

And maybe you're wondering, "why should I trust you to lead me on this
expedition?" Fair enough. Come along and see for yourself. Let me begin
with a few questions.

Which mountain are you actually climbing?
What would tell you it's the right one?
And if you discover it's the wrong one - what would you do?

It is May 2001.
I can see sunlight shining through the window, white flowers on the sill
leaning toward it, and images of 8,000 meter peaks smiling back at me
from the walls.
I can smell hot coffee steaming beside me.
I can hear the easy morning, a laugh in the corridor, then quick,
purposeful footsteps pounding toward my door.
I feel cold sweat on my skin as if the world is steady but something
inside me is already cracking, like a glacier shifting before it breaks.
I am in my thirties, with a well-curved body in a bright summer dress,
but no one who knew me ever mistook me for fragile. I am a **chamois**
through and through, an elegant mountain antelope, nimble on ridges,
stubborn in storms, happiest where the air thins. A woman of contrasts,
laughter and lipstick one day, ropes and crampons the next. A woman in
Munich wearing high heels on a mountain bike.

Then Bogdan bursts into my office like someone crashing into
basecamp at dawn, 1.90 meters tall, in his fifties, brown curls slightly
unruly, a three-day stubble on a face carved by wind. His grey shirt

clings from travel, his trekking trousers already dusted with the road. He radiates the kinetic energy of a man who's always halfway up a mountain, even when he's indoors.

If you need a movie reference think Liam Neeson in Taken, but with crampons and an ice axe. Charisma and danger in one.

Bogdan: "I got the permit for the First ascent for our 7000m peak in India. I want you to be part of my expedition. You could be the first woman on the summit. Believe me, this will be your legacy. You'll be remembered worldwide. You'd make history."

Simone: (Taking a deep breath) "I know. I know I could make it. But is this really my path? Is this what I should do with my life? The mountains already gave me everything - taught me about fear, about leadership, about bringing people home.

Changemakers

It breaks me to walk away. But it would cost me more to climb.
My path ends here, and I have to let it go." (I tell him with my eyes
filled with tears).

"Have you ever been on the road to success, with everything lined up,
the famous summit almost in reach, when suddenly you felt "this is not
my mountain? This path is over!"

What do you do? Push on, hoping it would feel right at the top?
Or step back, even if it meant leaving part of yourself behind.

I kept managing our extreme treks and expeditions in the company I´m
working for, pretending nothing had changed. Everyone knew my career
was over, everyone except me. Then I ended my 10 year-relationship with
Michael, a German mountain guide. It felt like an avalanche. I quit high-
altitude expeditions, hiding instead in seaside cliffs, pretending chalk
and sea breeze could cover the void. My life was falling apart, and the
tsunami was still to come.

It is a Monday morning in September 2001.

I step into the office of the CEO and Shareholder of the Market leader for
trekking and expeditions in the German-speaking region.

I can see stacks of papers, a framed photo with Sir Edmund Hillary, and
the empty chair I'm walking toward.

I can smell lemon cleaner, and that metallic hint that means a storm is
coming, only this one isn't on any weather chart.

He is already waiting for me, Andreas is in his mid forties, his legs
crossed, one foot bouncing nervously, I can hear his fingers tapping on
the wooden table like a metronome.

Andreas: "You went too far with the training of our Guides last weekend.
Fear, identity, boundaries, that's therapy. Not our job."

Simone: "Above 4,000 meters, pretending there's a line between personal and professional makes Guides fail. I'm not doing therapy, I'm teaching leadership under pressure. The same tools that bring a rope team back alive, naming the storm, probing crevasses, setting a turn-back time, are what our guides need."

Andreas: "Nice metaphor. But not our business. We sell trips, logistics, safety. Drop this idea." - (Silence)

Simone: "But... ahm...(my voice is thin and trembling) then I need to cut the rope. I quit, Andreas. I'll take this work on my own now, my expedition, my summit, no matter the risk."

The tsunami hit me, sudden, unstoppable. "Oh my Gosh, what did I just do?" But I had no choice, I had to quit my job.

This was my first expedition without a rope team, just me. Six months of self-leadership, day by day. I saw that every human already carries four tools to reach any summit: **Words, Thoughts, Emotions, Actions.** That was the birth of Human Technology.

Later came another truth, three levels of consciousness, and the superconscious awakens the genius in us all. I had touched it in the mountains, but only now did I recognise it.

From there came the **High IMPACT Leadership License.** Too many leaders ignore their own human technology, sacrificing health, neglecting wealth, trapped in layers of limitation.

That's the moment you stand alone on the glacier. No rope team. No fixed lines. Just you and your tools.

And maybe you've been there too, when no one else can carry you across. *"Which tools do you trust when the ground cracks under your feet?"*

Extracting the strategies I once used unconsciously was one climb. Building a business from nothing, that was steeper.

And the chorus came quickly,

Michael my ex-partner in life and in the mountains: "Your salary was among the highest. You coached guides, even families who lost loved ones. Not a single lawsuit. You throw it all away!

Anita a friend of mine told me: "You had the dream job - first ascents, treks, global partners. What could be better?"

My mother, close to tears, said: "I told everyone you will become the female Reinhold Messner, a famous star, and now, you are a nobody!"

Step by step I built a new basecamp, a small practice translating high-altitude disciplines into everyday leadership. At first individuals and couples, real lives at real edges. Then parents. Soon, managers, living at an altitude without leaving their desks.

The first success stories were written. The inefficient meetings of John F. became ascents with defined routes, not blind slogs. His work became a rope people could trust.

I watched how Peter D's depression lifts, momentum returned, and his KPIs not just met but surpassed. I still remember the first quantum leap, Christian A. made millions, yes, but more than that, he rerouted his whole life. Foot pain gone. Six nightly wake-ups turned into sleeping like a child.

I wasn't treating symptoms. We rebuilt his self-leadership, habits, decisions and stress. His body followed.

I didn't become the first woman on that Indian peak. Instead, I became the guide who helps others reach theirs, and return safely to what matters most. Do I regret saying no? I don't. Sometimes the bravest ascent is a well-chosen descent. The mountain I didn't climb gave me a clearer view, success isn't standing alone on a ridge; it's standing with a rope team that make high impact decisions because they learned to lead themselves first.

Today, all of this is distilled into the **High IMPACT Leadership License,** a path to empower yourself and your teams. Made for leaders, game changers, and future builders who want altitude without the oxygen mask, leading expeditions and climbing peaks called teams, targets, board rooms and tough conversations. This is where the journey becomes practical. Let me take you step by step into the **High IMPACT Leadership License.**

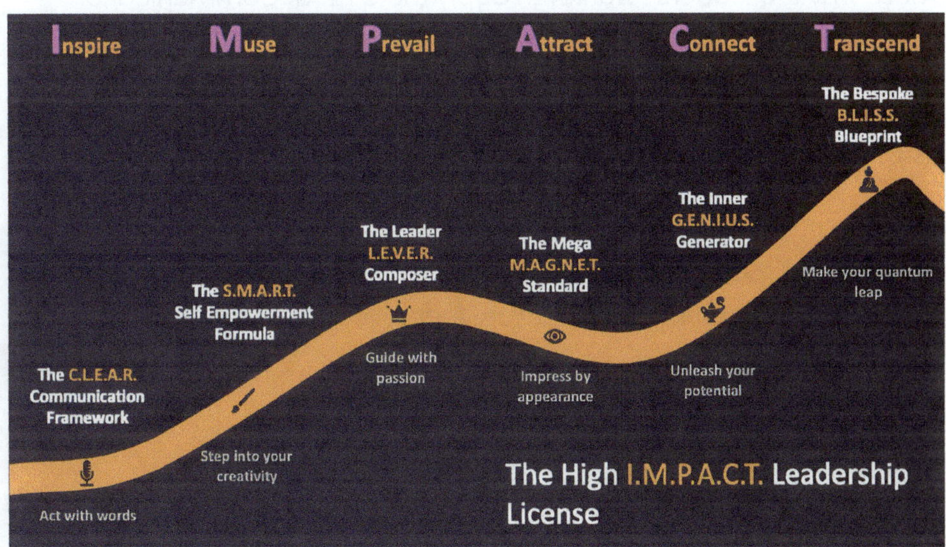

The High Impact Leadership License

Stage 1: Act with Words – Inspire

Every expedition begins with words: the calls across a ridge, the map briefing before the climb, the quiet reassurance on the rope.

Yet most managers overwhelm their teams with noise. The average person speaks about seven thousand words a day. The average manager? Between thirty and fifty thousand. That's six hours of monologue. Too many words, too little clarity. The result? Confusion, low quality, lost clients.

I once coached a director who proudly told me he "kept everyone informed" by sending daily emails. His team confessed they stopped reading them. He thought he was leading; in reality, he was burying his people in an avalanche of words.

Here's the truth: your words are your rope. They can secure trust - or they can tangle the entire team.

That's why the leaders I work with apply the C.L.E.A.R Communication Framework. They grow their people with words that empower and inspire, transform negativity into possibility, and run meetings that feel like summits reached together—not avalanches of slides. Productivity rises. Leaders gain not just digital followers on LinkedIn, but real-life loyalty. Sales increase naturally, because clarity always converts.

💡 *Reflection for you*: Before speaking, run it through three filters: Is it true? Can I say it positively? Is it necessary for the job?

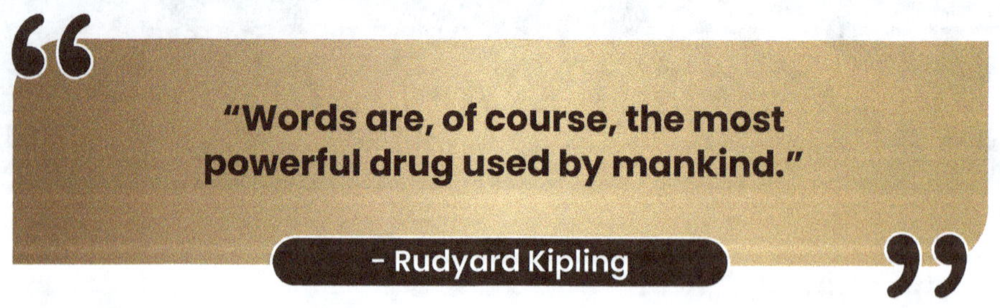

When you master words, you become more than a manager. You become an inspirer - a climber others trust to tie in with.

Stage 2: Step into Creativity - Muse

Sooner or later, the trail steepens. Logic alone won't get you across a crevasse. You need creativity - the ability to see a route where others see only a dead end.

But many leaders tell me:

> **"Simone, I'm rational all day. When I need creativity - for a pitch, a strategy, a solution - I can't just switch it on."**

So, they delay. Deadlines slip. Presentations bore. Stress builds.
Creativity isn't a luxury - it's the oxygen of innovation.
And it can be trained.

My clients practice The S.M.A.R.T. Self-Empowerment Formula mental procedures that unlock creativity in seconds.

Einstein himself relied on "thought experiments." The theory of relativity was born not in a lab, but in his imagination. Leaders can do the same.

One CEO dreaded presenting to investors. He claimed he "wasn't creative." We tried a simple exercise: Imagine it's one year later, and your investors are celebrating you. What exactly are they applauding? In minutes, his tone shifted from dry to inspired, When he finally stood in front of his investors, they felt that inspiration too."

💡 *Reflection for you:* Before your next strategy session, close your eyes. Imagine the project is already a wild success. Ask: What did we do differently to make it work?

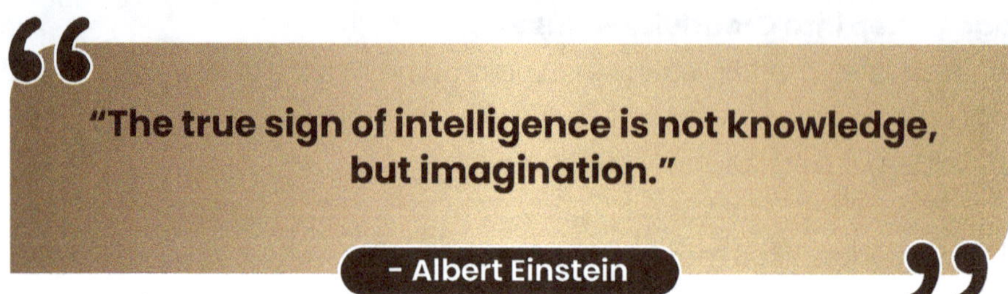

Stage 3: Guide with Passion – Prevail

Every climber faces storms. The question is not if emotions hit, but how you prevail when they do.

Far too many leaders still believe emotions have no place in business. So, they take one of two dangerous paths: the poker face, suppressing emotions until they collapse inside; or the floodgate, expressing everything and exhausting everyone. Both lead to what doctors' call "Manager's Disease": a list of symptoms like stress, high blood pressure, depression, burnout—even heart disease or stroke.

Science is clear: negative emotions release stress hormones that make us sick if unprocessed. Positive emotions, on the other hand, boost resilience and extend life expectancy.

One senior partner admitted his silence made people feel invisible. Another confessed his team feared his outbursts. Both were burning out. With The Leader L.E.V.E.R. Composer, they learned to let go of harmful emotions and generate positive ones — sometimes in the middle of a meeting. The change was visible: calmer breathing, clearer eyes, a room that felt safe again.

💡 *Reflection for you:* Next time stress hits, pause for thirty seconds. Ask yourself: What emotion would serve me better right now? Calm? Curiosity? Courage?

Decisions made in good mood are more successful, science has proven it. And a culture of smiles reduces sick leave, lowers turnover, and turns teams into rope parties that actually enjoy the climb.

When you prevail in this way, storms don't destroy your expedition — they test and strengthen it. Your rope team follows you with trust, knowing that even in chaos, you keep the line steady.

Stage 4: Impress by Appearance — Attract

Research by Albert Mehrabian showed that words account for only seven percent of impact. The rest is tone, body language, and presence. Yet many managers think appearance is only about a suit or a haircut. They forget that presence is also how you walk through the office, how you breathe when you enter, how you look at your people. Too often, leaders carry an invisible shield on their backs that says: 'Do Not Disturb.' The result? People stop approaching. Conversations shrink into rumours. Trust erodes. Careers derail.

But when leaders apply The Mega M.A.G.N.E.T. Standard, something shifts. They radiate confidence without arrogance. They attract top talent not through charisma alone, but through integrity — because they do what they say. They walk like climbers who know their rope is solid, and everyone senses it.

💡 *Reflection for you:* Before your next meeting, stop at the door. Plant your feet. Take a deep breath. Lift your chest. Step in as if you're tying the rope for the whole team.

On the rope, presence is the difference between panic and calm. In business, it's what turns a manager into a magnet.

Stage 5: Unleash Potential — Connect

The higher you climb, the more awareness and consciousness matter. Most managers operate on autopilot—guided by the subconscious, replaying fears and past experiences in reaction mode. This creates over-control, micromanagement, and stagnation. Teams suffocate. Relationships fracture.

Changemakers

Leaders who connect with their super-consciousness access something extraordinary: their inner genius. I call this The Inner G.E.N.I.U.S. Generator. And yes, there's a simple, step-by-step way to do it. We go into this in more detail at the High IMPACT Leadership Academy. Most managers lead as if they were navigating a glacier blindfolded. But when you connect with super-consciousness, it's like pulling off the blindfold and finally seeing the markers to cross safely.

A division head was notorious for micromanaging. Almost every decision had to go through him, and the business stalled. Through consciousness connection training, he shifted into leading from vision instead of fear. Within six months, not only did his business line grow, but his marriage—on the brink of collapse—began to heal.

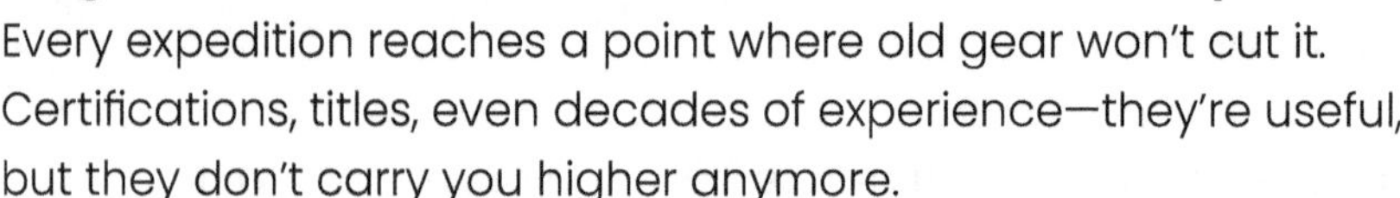 *Reflection for you:* Before deciding on something critical, ask: *Am I choosing from limitation, or from vision?*

On a glacier, this is the moment you trust the ground under your feet—and yourself—to find a safe crossing where no map exists. In leadership, it's the moment where potential turns into power.

Stage 6: Transcend Limits — Make Your Quantum Leap

Every expedition reaches a point where old gear won't cut it. Certifications, titles, even decades of experience—they're useful, but they don't carry you higher anymore.

Too many leaders remain stuck—new jobs, same problems, new partners, old conflicts. Different summit, same storm.

The way forward is leadership transformation. The Business Owners and Top Managers I work with use The B.L.I.S.S. Blueprint—a series of processes that rewire limitations into strengths, upgrade beliefs about energy and money, build a millionaire's mindset, and reframe relationships with statistics and probabilities so numbers no longer hold them back.

One entrepreneur had all the external signs of success: revenue in the millions, a corner office, recognition in the industry. Yet he confessed he felt trapped in a cage of golden bars. Through the B.L.I.S.S. Blueprint, he let go of old scripts around money and failure.

The result? Not just groundbreaking new visions, but genuine freedom—a deep sense of independence. He began investing in social projects, dancing again with his wife, even taking his son on expeditions. That was his quantum leap.

💡 *Reflection for you:* Write down the summit you're chasing. Then ask yourself: What limiting belief do I need to let go to get there?
The moment when the fixed ropes end, and you must climb on your own, skill and courage is where your leadership stops being only about you. It's when your limits dissolve and your journey becomes legacy.

If there is only one thing you carry with you from this climb, let it be this: Laughter is the best medicine.

Keep your rope team smiling, and you'll be a Game Changer—bringing Health, Wealth, and Happiness not only to yourself, but to everyone tied to your rope.

Simone Heinzelmann didn't start out brave. As a child, she hid under tables, too shy to even speak to neighbours. Years later, she would be clinging to icy ridges and gasping for air above 6,000 meters, on mountains that became mirrors of her inner fears. Living and traveling through Nepal, Bangkok, Singapore, Malaysia, and Japan transformed those outward expeditions into a journey of inner discovery.

Out of those lessons, Simone created the Human Technology Platform, her professional basecamp. Anchored by a degree in Business Administration, she launched her first brand, The High IMPACT Leadership License - a powerful fusion of business logic, extreme adventure, and Eastern wisdom.

Today, as an award-winning keynote speaker, executive coach, and founder, Simone guides leaders to transform fear into strength and pressure into clarity. Her mission is simple but profound: to help people climb their own summits through **People Powered Performance -** because even superheroes need a team.

Your Basecamp Awaits
Scan the code to join my 90-minute live session. Upgrade your human technology, choose your route, and climb without burning out. High Impact Leadership starts here.

Scan the QR code for More!

CHAPTER 6

GRIP TO GROWTH

THE UNSPOKEN PATH TO HEALING

"When we grip the roots of our pain with courage, we discover the hidden wisdom to grow beyond it - healing is not loud, it is the quiet power of presence."

- Rick Charlton
• • •

Have you ever wondered how to help when someone tells you "I'm fine" and you know it really means "I'm broken"?

Let me take you back to December 2009, a road traffic collision in the north of England. I can smell the blood first. That unforgettable scent of blood in traumatic vehicle accidents is sharp, metallic, and suffused with an eerie stillness. It's not just the iron-rich scent of haemoglobin that hits you; it's the way it blends with burnt rubber, leaked fuel, and the acrid tang of fractured plastic and metal. That coppery odour becomes thick and humid when mixed with adrenaline, shock, and heat. There's also a psychological layering to it. In the immediacy of trauma, the scent carries weight, registering not just in the nose but somewhere deeper, evoking primal alertness or grief. It's not unlike a forge, metallic, heated, and hanging in the air like something working but broken at the same time.

I can see twisted metal and shattered glass glinting under flashing beacons that cut through the haze, blue, strobing against the pale faces and wreckage, and the stark brightness of the portable scene lights. The airbags are deflated, smeared red and white, crumpled like used tissues. Debris is scattered like fragments of a story violently torn apart, wheel trims, personal items, ripped upholstery. I see people moving erratically, some helping, some stunned, others just frozen. Steam rises from engines, mingling with cold December drizzling rain.

I can hear sirens swelling and fading, an auditory lighthouse drawing responders in. Panic-sharp cries and strained voices form a human soundscape of urgency and confusion. The shouts of responders use clipped, command tones: *"Clear the area!" "Can you hear me?"* The crackle of radios relay instructions in clipped bursts. Groans from twisted metal, cooling and shifting after the force of impact. Footsteps crunching over broken glass and gravel, each one deliberate, invasive. It's a soundscape not unlike war or collapse, every noise a punctuation mark in a narrative of sudden trauma.

Changemakers

I arrived and stepped into the scene as the fire service commander
with a mix of instinct, training, and a burdensome clarity. Two fire
crews are already here and have started work supervised by the crew
commanders, waiting for me to take overall incident command.

I feel hyper-focused urgency; my senses narrow not to shut out chaos,
but to interpret it fast. I'm absorbing the layout, risks, positions of
casualties, vehicle types, and spill patterns. The weight of responsibility
bears down. Every decision could mean life or death. I feel the invisible
pull of command, the need to protect, to lead, to act. I also feel the
tug of empathic tension deep in my stomach. There's the horror of
this scene, yes, for me this is normal, this is my work! But I also feel the
need to shield my crews emotionally while keeping them effective. I'm
subconsciously registering the human moral cost, then boxing
it away for later.

Almost like magic, I'm overcome with a familiar calculated calm ....
practiced, almost ritualistic. Calm is currency in chaos. I speak clearly,
not loudly, with eye contact, giving quick assessments, triaging with
voice and gestures.

Then the moral gravity hits. Not just the five people trapped in the taxi,
but *I realise that I know the taxi driver;* his son plays rugby with my own
boy. He doesn't recognise me in my fire kit and helmet; he's in a bad
way. Then there's the young lad trapped in the other crumpled car,
disfigured by the impact, wheezing to take a breath… there's a visceral
ache that lodges deep and quiet. I know this job's different to all the
others, the effects of this one won't surface until later when the job is done.

My crew's safety is paramount. I feel every risk as a possible misstep with
real consequences. My internal monologue is echoing "Absorb. Decide.
Move. Debrief later.", layered beneath is my personal mantra: "do what
you can, with what you have got, to help as many as you can". This isn't
just command; it's communion with chaos.

A crew manager I know approaches. "Rick… the lad in the second car… he's John's nephew". "What?" My eyes flick briefly toward the wreckage. Recognition flickers, then solidifies. "John was meant to be on tonight. Christmas party. Switched shifts last-minute". "Shit… I trained John from scratch. Watched him find his feet in this job. God". My voice trails off, the professional shell cracking under a personal quake. There's a moment of silence, just the distant thrum of a siren and the snap of a cutting tool. "He'll carry that. For years". "We all will".

I now experience a collision between duty and relationship. Reality distorts when faces in the wreckage relate to people from memory. I feel a deep moral ache. The "what if" drills into my mind, had the party not happened, had the shift not changed. I'm overcome with protective sorrow, wanting to shield John from the knowledge, yet knowing it'll find him soon enough. Amidst it all, I need to stay focused, to lead with clarity while carrying personal grief silently.

This moment marks a fracture line between command and humanity. That moment… sharp, aching, defiant, is the kind of truth that doesn't fit neatly into any protocol. A rupture in the rhythm of command, and I've stepped into it not just as a leader, but as a human tethered to duty and heart.

The metal groans as the cutters finish their work, peeling the roof away like the lid of a beans tin. Steam rises from fractured radiator. The boy's body lies crumpled inside, lifeless yet not gone, the air around him thick with the scent of fuel and coolant. I climb in, boots slipping on the wet, grinding glass and grit, settling gently onto the dashboard. It's a break from command protocol, but no voice objects. They see it in my face. This isn't interference. This is presence. "Stay with us, lad. You're not alone. You're safe now". My hands hold his head, opening his airway, every rasp from his lungs a thunderclap inside my own chest. Unconscious, yet still fighting. I speak quietly, not to wake him, to anchor him. Thoughts of my own children at home tucked up safe in bed are quickly subdued and suppressed. *"You're doing fine. We're right here. Your uncle trained with me… he's family. Just stay a little longer".*

Changemakers

The paramedics slide the board in. I shift carefully, lifting with them, making space only when the last strap clicks. I hold his hand. "Squeeze, lad. Show me you're still in this". His fingers curl faintly around mine, tremoring, not with strength, but with will. "That's it. Hold on. Grip hard. We're nearly there". I'm walking now, fast, toward the ambulance. The scene around me blurs. Lights strobe on my visor, but my eyes never leave his face. As I step up into the back, his hand tightens one last time. "We've got you. We've got you". And then, the grip fades. A silence worse than sirens. He dies holding my hand. And I don't let go.

In certain Indigenous traditions, holding someone physically during transition is sacred. It's believed the last breath travels not just through the mouth, but through the skin. That breath doesn't vanish; it transfers. My hand became more than a conduit; it became the bridge between presence and passing. In that instant, I wasn't just a firefighter or commander; I was the grip bearer, who steadies the soul at the edge. Little did I know, this was to become a metaphor for my life's work and purpose:

"The role of a leader isn't only to command during crisis, but to offer the last grip in moments of passage, whether from trauma to recovery, chaos to clarity, or pain to peace".

Just as traditional healers might sit beside those crossing thresholds, I was within the breach, holding what protocol usually avoids, the raw truth of closeness. I didn't instruct from a distance; I entered the moment, became its witness and its weight-bearer.

The Fracture Begins: After the Incident

In the aftermath of that Christmas night, something cracked, not loudly, but relentlessly. Each emergency call became a summon to relive that boy's final breath. My body suited up, my voice commanded, my boots still walked into chaos, but inside, a quiet dread nested. PTSD crept in slowly, wearing the face of insomnia, hypervigilance, and emotional numbness. I found myself replaying scenes not just in memory, but in muscle, clenched fists, shallow breathing, a thudding heart for no reason but ghosts. Frustration was high: "I've been a soldier, I've been to war! This shouldn't be bothering me so much!".

I began to dread the very thing I'd once been forged for, the sound of the pager, the smell of smoke, the weight of leadership. Protocol was no longer a shield, but a trapdoor. I was performing the motions, but my soul was elsewhere, dragged back into that crushed vehicle every time I saw a young person driving or heard the stuttered rasp of strained breath.

Eventually, the uniform came off. Not as triumph, but as quiet surrender.

The Illusion of Escape: Ten Years of Masked Success

I moved into a different industry, hoping that distance would bring healing. The salary grew, the title gleamed, and from the outside, I looked like a man who'd mastered transition. But internally, the mask tightened. Corporate success offered no balm for soul-wounds. My marriage ended, communication frayed, intimacy hollowed out. I was present but partitioned. I was even homeless for a while, and nobody knew, the mask was on tight. Friends praised my resilience, but they never met the sleepless version of me or the one who flinched at loud noises and silent thoughts. Despair became quiet companionship. I didn't speak to it, but I carried it. Hidden behind PowerPoints and leadership meetings was a man who'd once held a dying boy's hand and never let go of that final grip.

The Turning Point: Meeting Andy

Then came Andy, also a former firefighter. A Trauma Incident Reduction (TIR) facilitator. His journey was similar and relatable, his own path decided in the aftermath of 9/11 where he was recovering the deceased from the rubble of the World Trade Centre in New York. He didn't just talk about trauma; he invited me to trace it, sit with it, dialogue with it. Something opened, not immediately, but with enough space for curiosity. I qualified as a coach, studied trauma, mental health, and the scaffolding of recovery.

Coaching became more than a profession; it became a language to reclaim the unspeakable. I found that my pain had grammar, my memories had rhythm, and my experiences had tools embedded in them. I wasn't broken. I was coded for growth, but my system hadn't been shown how.

The Kalahari Reckoning: Journey into the wilderness

I grew up in Botswana, Southern Africa, and I decided I needed to return home to find myself. I stepped into Botswana's central Kalahari Desert, alone, unconnected by technology, with no duty, just silence and presence. Alone with the bush, the animals, the wind, and the stars, gazing into my campfire, I unlearned the noise of 'leadership-as-performance'. I remembered myself not as a victim of trauma, but as a witness to sacred passage. The desert didn't offer escape; it offered 'mirror and medicine'. Each footprint became a metaphor. Each dawn a reminder. There, stripped of performance and rank, the clarity emerged, "post-traumatic stress is a wound. Post-traumatic growth is a vow". I saw myself not just as a survivor, but as a 'torchbearer,' ... forged in war and in fire, whose path now led not into danger but into healing others.

The Meeting with the San Bushman Elder

Around a low fire that crackled like time itself, I spoke with an elderly San bushman guide, his eyes as weathered and watchful as the desert stones. He shared ancient wisdom that trauma leaves spiritual echoes, not just psychological scars. That healing is not achieved by erasing pain, but by witnessing it communally, rhythmically, with breath and ritual. That even sorrow must dance, through stories, songs, and silence. "In our way," he said, "the soul staggers until it finds its tribe. Then it begins to walk again".

This conversation didn't just resonate, it reframed everything. I saw the Western model of trauma as linear, but the Indigenous way was cyclical, ritualised, and relational.

Reclaimed Purpose: Turning Pain into a Compass

My professional journey from soldier to firefighter to coach taught me to stand in transitions, hold the "grip others can't". I create frameworks of resilience, inspired by my revelation. In the Kalahari's deep hush, where silence speaks in ancient rhythms, I found not just solitude, but revelation. Beneath the Baobabs and beneath my own skin, I learned that trauma isn't a rupture to fix, it's a passage to honour.

The Shift to Coaching and Facilitation

Returning from Botswana, I decided to transform my trauma instead of escaping it. I trained as a Trauma-Informed Mindset Coach and TIR Facilitator. I studied Shinrin Yoku (Forest Bathing) enabling well-being through nature. I approached coaching with the resilience of a warrior, the wisdom of an elder, the structure of a clinician. Integrating Indigenous wisdom, modern coaching psychology, and Applied Metapsychology to create a holistic healing framework.

Here's what I learned, a beautiful irony.

This isn't therapy, it's structured, person-led resolution. No digging. No diagnosis. Just a safe way to revisit trauma until the emotional charge dissolves. Whilst backed by modern neuroscience and operational rigour, its philosophy is ancient.

Changemakers

In African cultures, they say, "Ubuntu." I am because we are.
Healing is communal. In the Zulu tradition, after a traumatic event,
the village gathers. There is ritual, rhythm, and release through
movement, music, and storytelling. The community don't analyse the
pain; they witness it. The Dagara people of Burkina Faso perform grief
rituals to release unspoken sorrow. The burden is shared, not buried.

In Native American cultures, ceremonies like the "wiping of tears" provide
sacred structure for mourning and moving forward. In talking circles,
people speak without interruption, because being heard is the first step
to being healed. What these traditions knew, and what my approach
affirms, is this, healing doesn't happen through labels. Healing happens
through process, presence, and permission.

Then, in the universe's mystical way, a LinkedIn message from a Kenyan
practitioner, Munene, led me to observe anti-poaching rangers in Kenya.
I saw their trauma, flashbacks, hyper-vigilance, and grief from armed
confrontations and moral injury which mirrored my own experiences. By
sharing models from my private practice, I provided visible relief to the
rangers. This inspired us to co-found Strong Ranger Resilience (SRR) CIC,
a non-profit dedicated to supporting rangers with trauma recovery.

After returning to the UK, my experiences in Kenya and my personal
journey became the catalyst for my private practice. I recognised that
trauma is everywhere, affecting people from all walks of life, including
high-profile professionals like celebrities, sportspeople, and ordinary
individuals. However, when people attempt to discuss trauma, they are
often met with resistance and phrases like, "we're fine," or "move on".
Often, facilitation is dismissed as "therapy talk" that's unnecessary for
those who are considered "tough". My experience is that this scepticism
ignores the unspoken burdens and quiet devastation that trauma
inflicts, fracturing lives beneath a polished exterior.

My journey, from holding a dying boy's hand at a car crash to guiding
rangers in Africa, taught me how trauma hides behind brave faces.

This journey inspired the creation of my system, a unique branded solution for healing that helps people move from survival to growth.

My mission is to help people heal from trauma using the 'Rising P.H.O.E.N.I.X. Framework,' a seven-stage model for personal and communal growth. Combining Indigenous wisdom, mindset coaching, and Applied Metapsychology, it's designed for anyone whose courage is unspoken, pain unseen. My vow is to create a "sacred space" for people to be held, heard, and healed, guiding them from post-traumatic stress to post-traumatic growth.

Before I take you through my system, lets address the question I asked at the start, how do you help someone who says, "I'm fine," but is "broken"? Well, 'I'm fine' is a survival skill, not a status report. Helping someone in this state is like tracking a shadow animal, you must walk alongside it rather than chase it. The deepest form of help is to reconnect them to their "sacred breath" and honour their pain as part of their soul, rather than trying to fix them.

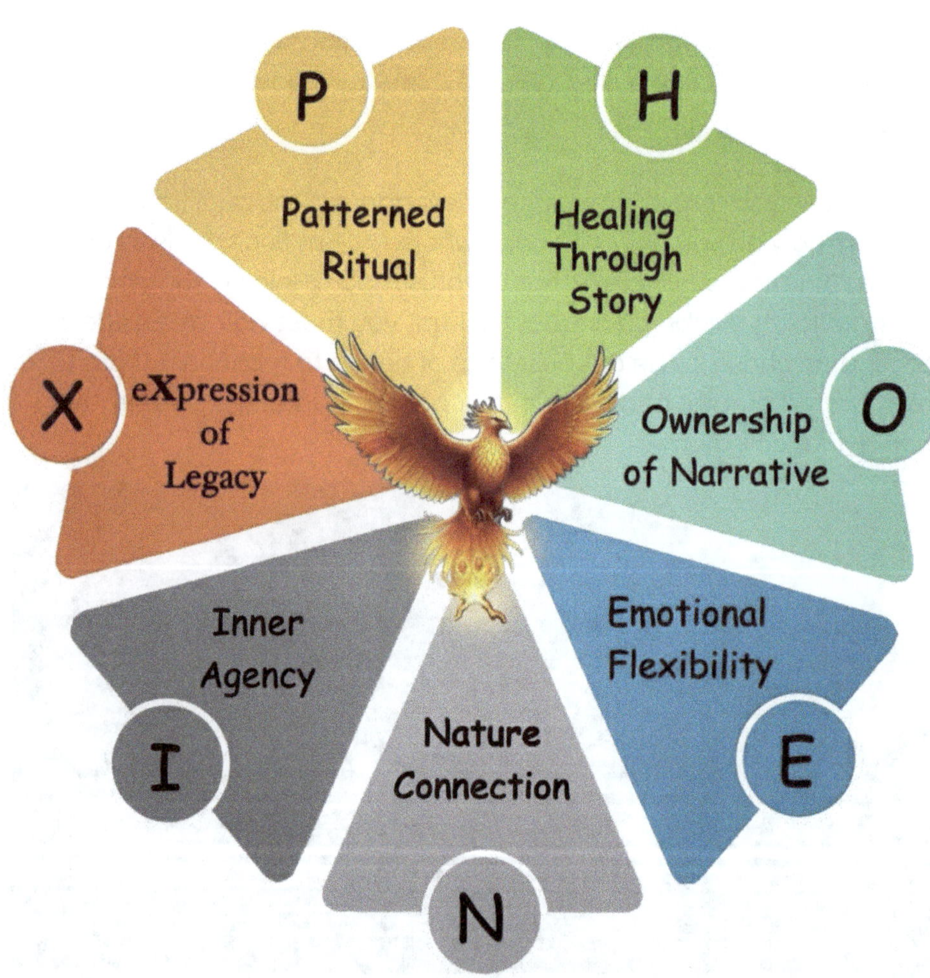

P
Patterned Ritual
H
Healing Through Story
O
Ownership of Narrative
E
Emotional Flexibility
N
Nature Connection
I
Inner Agency
X
eXpression of Legacy

The 'Rising P.H.O.E.N.I.X. Framework'

Patterned Ritual & Presence: Addresses how traditional talking therapy often fails because trauma is a non-verbal, bodily experience. The framework uses patterned practices to help clients regain control and regulate emotions.

Healing Through Story & Symbol: Recognises that trauma shatters a person's life story. Clients use the **'3 Mountains Story Model'** to create a new, organised narrative and use symbols to process feelings.

Ownership of Narrative: Focuses on helping clients move beyond being defined by a "trauma story" by using the **'Ownership Activator'** to integrate past events into a new narrative of resilience and meaning.

Emotional Flexibility & Expression: Uses the **'Mind Gym'** to help clients overcome emotional constriction and a cycle of fear or numbness.

Nature Connection & Non-Linear Wisdom: Counters the rigid thinking associated with trauma by using the **'Wilderness shift system'** to help clients connect with nature's non-linear wisdom and process emotions without words.

Inner Agency & Integration: Addresses the loss of control and fractured self that trauma causes. The **'Agency Integrator System'** helps clients develop a sense of inner agency and accept different parts of themselves.

eXpression of Legacy & Communal Witnessing: Counters the isolation of privatised trauma. Clients learn that communal healing and creating a legacy are essential for transforming pain into something that benefits others, allowing them to move from surviving to thriving.

Rick has over 30 years of experience in leadership, operations, and coaching within diverse and challenging environments. His career spans roles in the British Army, the Fire and Rescue Service, HM Government, Corporate leadership, and supporting Anti-Poaching Operations in Africa. After years of silently struggling with PTSD, Rick's journey led him back to his childhood home in Botswana, where he fused his personal experiences with Indigenous wisdom, modern psychology, and Applied Metapsychology. Today, he helps people across all walks of life move from post-traumatic stress to post-traumatic growth, creating a "sacred space" for them to be held, heard, and healed.

Scan the QR code for More!

CHAPTER 7
FROM
INVISIBLE TO
IRRESISTIBLE
THE GEMS WITHIN EVERY WOMAN

BUILDING AN AUTHENTIC PERSONAL BRAND THAT SHINES AND ATTRACTS FROM THE INSIDE OUT

"In a marketplace full of manufactured personas that profit from our insecurity, authenticity has become the rarest and most valuable currency"

– Marianna Penna

...

"I am exhausted!

I've worked hard for years, built a career, raised a family, created a home. I've achieved what I've always dreamed of, yet I still feel incomplete. In midlife, demands pile up and expectations grow heavier. On the other side, energy, joy, spontaneity, everything seems to vanish. Bit by bit, I feel I have lost myself.

I've been looking toward a brighter future, hoping for comfort, while losing sight of the present, the very moment where my true self resides. In chasing success and validation outside myself, I've overlooked the most important part: my own soul. I poured energy into every role, every demand, yet left myself thirsty. And if I cannot truly see and honour the gems within me, how can I expect the world to see them?

And my business? I feel like I'm losing my mind. I am a leader, running my own company. People rely on me. I feel lonely and overwhelmed on this journey. I should have all the answers. I work hard, long hours; I read business books, follow trends, push myself to be resilient, capable, invincible. On top of that, I'm told I must look polished, fit, glamorous, and socially active. That's supposedly what it takes to be seen as an expert, a woman of influence.

Since Covid the market feels unpredictable, almost hostile. Social media demands endless performance: content, podcasts, books, events. Push, push, push. Run, run, run. Fast, fast, fast! How long can I keep going like this before I break?

AI is everywhere, and I know it's an opportunity. Yet I feel unsure how to use it while remaining authentic. I want to come across as genuine, but I don't know how. And honestly, I feel too old for social media. I dislike how I look; I'm uncomfortable on camera. I check every detail before posting, but even then, I wonder, "how can I attract new clients if I don't look great, if my script isn't perfect, and if, even when I put myself out there, I still don't feel seen?"

Changemakers

I search for work-life balance. Health gurus preach balance. Nutritionists promise quick fixes. Coaches demand discipline. Marketing experts shout consistency. I feel pulled in every direction, tumbling inside a washing machine. While I spin, my message blurs, my presence weakens, my brand loses coherence.

My mentor tells me, 'Focus. Not every door needs to be opened.' Yet I chase every opportunity, thinking one might finally lead to success. In that chase I create only stress and distraction.

STOP. I've had enough! Sometimes I think I should quit. Why stretch myself thin, trying to be everything to everyone, when the reward is stress, sleepless nights, and a business that feels like a burden and doesn't make the money I wish for?

So, I stand here asking: "Who am I? What do I want? What do I need?"

How often do women talk to themselves this way?
I know exactly how it sounds; I've lived it myself.

The Weight of Being Too Human

Naples, September 1989.
The September sun streams through the tall windows of our chemistry classroom, casting golden rectangles across worn wooden desks.
I'm fifteen, chatting with a classmate about our holidays,
when suddenly, "PENNA!"

Professoressa "Freeda," our chemistry teacher, moves through the room like a predator. Short, angular, short steel-grey hair pulled back, highlighting her sharp cheekbones and prominent, aquiline nose. Her black-rimmed glasses magnify eyes that never seem to blink. She wears the same dark wool suit every day, smelling faintly of stale coffee and antiseptic.

Every movement is deliberate, slow, terrifyingly controlled. Her voice cuts through conversation like a blade. Every head turns. The hum of students fades into silence.

She has asked a question about chemical bonds to Miss "Rainbow", a classmate of mine repeating the year. Frozen beside me, Miss "Rainbow" stares at her textbook. Professoressa "Freeda's" gaze sweeps the room, sharp and calculating.

"Penna, as you are human, because you are just human," she continues, approaching my desk, "help Miss "Rainbow"!"

The message is unmistakable: Miss "Rainbow" is hopeless. Me? Merely human, mediocre - just enough to highlight her failure.

Time stops. Twenty-five pairs of eyes fix on me. Blood rushes to my cheeks. Her lips curl in a faint, cold smile. She has made her point: "You are ordinary. Nothing special. Just human. Nothing more."

But what if those moments when we're told we're "human" "too emotional," or "too much", are actually revealing the precious materials from which our authentic brands will be built?

The Clash with Convention

London, February 2020.
A West London studio buzzes with nervous energy. I adjust my blazer, feeling a flutter of creative excitement. As the newly appointed female Managing Partner of a tax law firm, I hold what some might call an "unusual" vision, professionals can have personality; and expertise doesn't require emotional sterility. Today's team photoshoot is not about headshots, it's about showing that humanity and authority can coexist. He doesn't just walk in, he arrives. His shoes click against the studio floor like a gavel declaring judgment before anyone else can speak. His navy suit is cut so sharply it could cross-examine you; his tie is knotted with surgical precision, his confident, daring smile reveals teeth of dazzling

white that amplify his proud gaze — as though even gravity wouldn't dare argue with him. Determination radiates from him, but not the quiet, steady kind, it's the I've-already-won-before-you-open-your-mouth kind. His chin tilts a fraction too high, the universal sign for "I don't take advice, I give it." Mr."I Know Best," the Senior Partner, steps into the spotlight first.

The photographer asks: "What's your guilty pleasure? What makes you human outside legal credentials?"

Mr. "I Know Best," smirks, leaning into the lens with the confidence of a man who thinks the world is his jury: "I like sex and alcohol!"

The words drop like an unredacted footnote in a Supreme Court ruling. The room bursts out laughing, not because it's funny, but because he expects it to be. He revels in the reaction, eyes twinkling with the self-assuredness of someone convinced their wit is as bulletproof as their litigation skills.

But I don't laugh. Weeks of creative thought dissolve into a cheap punchline.
The sting is familiar — my work, my worth, reduced once again.

"Stop!" I say, steady. Inside, I'm screaming. "This is about showing who we are professionally, can't you see that?"

He waves me off casually, like a judge striking irrelevant evidence from the record: "Oh, come on. You're too serious. This is boring, and the campaign is a waste of time. You and your crazy ideas, this is going nowhere."

There it is. "Crazy ideas!" The same dismissal I've heard 30 years ago. What if the very qualities the world discourages you from expressing sensitivity, empathy, 'crazy' creativity, are actually raw gems waiting to become your greatest professional assets?

When Pressure Creates Brilliance

In that studio, watching my vision crumble, I had what I call my "Diamond Moment", a flash of clarity: *"I refuse to be squeezed into something that does not belong to me. I want to express my worth, be truly seen, appreciated, and build a business grounded in my own unique assets. I will uncover my strengths, reveal my gems, and build upon them!"*

That moment changed everything. I realised that the **qualities the world often tells us to hide, empathy, creativity, humanity, are actually the raw gems of our personal brand.** Gems that, when uncovered and polished, become the foundation for a business that is not just visible, but magnetic and successful.

Women today are building businesses faster than ever, yet many crumble inside. For decades, society has told them that, "empathy is weakness, creativity is impractical, and humanity does not belong in the business world." Now, paradoxically, authenticity is demanded, yet the very traits that make women extraordinary are often hidden, suppressed, or dismissed.

Hiding behind an image is exhausting and damaging. When you lose yourself, your personal brand, a reflection of who you truly are, becomes hollow. Masks crack, revealing doubt, exhaustion, and disillusionment. Without an authentic brand, business falters. Clients don't just buy services, they buy you. So, when "you" is hidden, opportunities slip by, and influence remains limited. Personal and professional are inseparable; your brand is not an accessory, it is the engine of **visibility, authority, and growth.**

This is where **brand clarity** becomes critical. Your brand is not just what you do, it is **who you are.** When your unique qualities are uncovered, refined, and expressed, you stop chasing opportunities and begin attracting them. A polished, authentic brand shines like a beacon, drawing the right clients, collaborators, and growth toward you. **Pressure doesn't destroy, it reveals.**

Changemakers

Every role, responsibility, doubt, and triumph applies pressure. Like ordinary stones transformed into diamonds, rubies, and emeralds, these pressures shape your hidden gems. Your personal brand journey mirrors this process: discover, align, and polish who you already are. The challenges you've faced, the doubts you've endured, and the "crazy" ideas you've been told to abandon are the very materials that will make your brand unique, powerful, and irresistible.

This is where authenticity becomes your compass. It is not a strategy, it is your essence revealed. When embraced fully, authenticity transforms these raw materials into a personal brand that doesn't just reflect who you are, it propels your business forward. Your story, values, and strengths become a magnet, naturally attracting opportunities, recognition, and influence.

And to guide this transformation, I built **The Brand YOU GemsCraft Journey ™** a step-by-step journey that helps women uncover, align, and polish their unique gems so their authentic brand can shine brilliantly in the marketplace.

So, the question is no longer, *"Should I quit?"*

The real question is, "Am I ready to uncover my gems and let them shine?"

Your journey to build a personal brand with authenticity begins here. Below is an overview of the precious recious journey, highlighting the common challenges women face in building their personal brand, how our solutions address them, and the benefits they deliver.

Shine from the inside out. The Brand YOU GemsCraft Journey ™.
Every woman carries her own gems, unique and precious. This is where my **Brand YOU GemsCraft Journey ™** begins, seven gems, seven steps to help women create a personal brand from Essence to Brilliance. Each gem represents a part of you, that pressure, and life, that needs to be crafted.

Each one is waiting to be discovered, crafted, and polished until your authentic brand shines.

Balance is essential in the professional life of women. It addresses the female struggle working from the outside-in. That is why I've integrated **the chakra system principles** into the **Brand YOU GemsCraft Journey™** because building a business isn't just strategy, it's energy alignment. When your root (security) is unstable, you hustle from fear. When your heart (connection) is blocked, your message falls flat. When your crown (vision) is ignored, your brand feels soulless. True personal branding isn't about adding layers, it's about removing them until your energy, values, and vision align. Work-life balance isn't a luxury; in today's fast-paced, demanding work world, it's the foundation of sustainable growth. The journey covers the seven-energy centres that when aligned, create harmony and flow. But I've translated these esoteric concepts into practical personal branding terms that resonate with accomplished women who don't have time for just abstract theory.

The Brand YOU GemsCraft Journey ™ has a diamond shape, with the seven gems placed along its structure representing your journey from Essence, where you boldly embrace who you truly are, to Brilliance, where your authentic self shines fully. At the base, you have three gems representing your inner foundation. At the peak, three gems representing your outer expression. And running horizontally through the centre, the crucial fourth gem that bonds inner and outer into authentic alignment.

Ruby (Root Chakra) – **Boldness: The Discovery Truth Ruby™**
Problem: Many women start their journey feeling disconnected from who they truly are. They mimic others' success, follow trends, or present a curated version of themselves that doesn't reflect their authentic essence. Too often, their personal brand and external style – from brand visuals to personal style – are misaligned, making their communication inconsistent and less trustworthy. This lack of coherence weakens their presence and confuses their audience about who they truly are.

Challenges: Confusion about core values, lack of clarity in identity, and difficulty distinguishing themselves from peers. Pressure to "fit in" overrides their intuition and voice, leading to inconsistency between who they are and how they present themselves to the world.

Consequences: Without a solid, grounded foundation, personal branding feels hollow. Women often experience imposter syndrome, inconsistency in messaging, and low visibility because their brand is not anchored in authenticity or expressed with stylistic coherence.

Solution: **The Discovery Truth Ruby™** methodology focuses on **Knowing Your Essence.** By exploring life experiences, values, and unique strengths, women uncover what makes them genuinely different - not superficially unique. This is about **embodying authenticity** in every aspect of communication, from tone of voice to visual and personal style, ensuring every expression reflects their true self.

Advantage: A strong Ruby foundation ensures that all branding and style decisions - from messaging and design to dress and presentation - are **authentically aligned.** This deep coherence between inner essence and outer expression builds **trust, magnetism, and unmistakable presence,** allowing women to communicate with precision and confidence while radiating a consistent, authentic style that sets them apart.

Carnelian (Sacral Chakra) – Bloom: The Creative Flow Carnelian™

Problem: Women often suppress their creativity or dismiss their innovative ideas as "too risky," "impractical," or "crazy." They feel pressure to conform to conventional expectations.

Challenges: Fear of judgment, self-censorship, lack of confidence in creative ideas, and difficulty expressing individuality in a crowded marketplace.

Consequences: Suppressed creativity leads to brand stagnation, loss of differentiation, and missed opportunities to stand out. Unique approaches remain hidden, leaving women invisible among competitors.

Solution: Carnelian helps **Ignite Your Creativity.** The methodology transforms ideas into actionable brand differentiators. It encourages discovering signature problem-solving styles, unique voices, and innovative approaches that make the brand memorable.

Advantage: Creative expression becomes a competitive edge. Women learn to leverage their originality, turning unconventional ideas into strategic opportunities that set their brand apart.

**Citrine (Solar Plexus Chakra) – Belief: The Core Differentiator Citrine™
Problem:** Many capable women struggle to articulate what makes their product or service truly unique. Even with exceptional skills and knowledge, they find it difficult to craft a compelling value proposition or package their offerings in a way that stands out in a crowded market. Self-doubt and imposter syndrome often amplify this challenge, making it hard to claim authority and show the world why they matter.

Challenges: Women may have a wealth of expertise but hesitate to define a signature methodology or approach. Fear of being "too visible," uncertainty about differentiation, and lack of confidence in promoting their unique strengths can prevent them from creating an irresistible offer that attracts clients, collaborators, or leadership opportunities.

Consequences: Without a clear, differentiated offering, their expertise can go unnoticed. Opportunities are missed, and even highly skilled women may be overlooked or undervalued. Their brand and impact remain underdeveloped, limiting growth and influence.

Solution: Citrine helps women step into their power by clarifying what sets them apart. It guides them to define a unique point of view, craft a distinctive methodology, and package their offerings in a way that is compelling and irresistible. By addressing imposter syndrome and building confidence and self-belief, women can sustain visibility, communicate authority, and stand out in their field.

Advantage: A strong, differentiated brand naturally attracts attention. Confidence and clarity turn expertise into recognised thought leadership, drawing clients, collaborators, and opportunities while establishing a powerful market presence.

**Emerald (Heart Chakra) – Bond: The Evergreen Relationship Emerald™
Problem:** Women are not purely transactional; they naturally seek meaningful, human connections. However, this strength can sometimes blur the boundaries between personal and professional relationships, making it harder to Make objective, impactful business decisions.

They deeply value empathy in business but often struggle to channel it in a way that nurtures sustainable, balanced relationships.

Challenges: Difficulty balancing self-interest with others' needs, challenges in fostering trust, and lack of community-building skills.

Consequences: Relationships feel shallow or short-lived, limiting referral opportunities, client loyalty, and long-term business growth. The brand may be seen as cold or impersonal.

Solution: Emerald guides women to Grow Sustainably Through Relationship Building and Community. It teaches how to convert empathy into a strategic advantage, building authentic connections aligned with shared values rather than temporary gains.

Advantage: Strong relational networks increase brand loyalty, referrals, and long-term opportunities. Empathy-driven marketing makes the brand magnetic and human-centered.

Sapphire (Throat Chakra) – Brightness: The Signature Message Sapphire™
Problem: Many women struggle to communicate their value effectively. Messaging can feel inconsistent, diluted, or disconnected from personal authenticity.

Challenges: Difficulty finding a confident voice, lack of storytelling techniques, and fear of being misunderstood or judged.

Consequences: Weak communication diminishes credibility, lowers engagement, and prevents a brand from being recognised in the marketplace. Potential clients may fail to grasp the brand's unique value.

Solution: Sapphire focuses on Confident Communication. It coordinates inner truth with outer expression, helping women develop signature phrases, storytelling methods, and communication frameworks, along with presentation skills for different media, that amplify authenticity.

Advantage: A clear, consistent voice elevates brand recognition, builds trust, and ensures messaging resonates with the right audience. Communication becomes a powerful tool to attract and inspire.

Amethyst (Third Eye Chakra) – Balance: The Amplified Authority Voice Amethyst™

Problem: Many women have valuable expertise and insights but struggle to share their message consistently and effectively. Even when they know their vision, translating it into content that reaches the right audience across multiple platforms - audio, video, blogs, podcasts, books - can feel overwhelming.

Challenges: Difficulty in defining a signature voice, uncertainty about which channels to use, and lack of confidence in producing or distributing content strategically. Women may also feel scattered, unsure how to package their ideas into formats that attract and engage their target audience.

Consequences: Without a clear multi-channel content strategy, their expertise can go unnoticed. Messages may be inconsistent, reach may be limited, and opportunities for influence, leadership, and growth may be missed.

Solution: Amethyst guides women to amplify their authority by helping them publish content strategically across formats that resonate with their audience. From blogs to podcasts, videos, and books, women learn to package their insights into engaging, accessible, and compelling content, ensuring their message reaches the right people in the right way.

Advantage: By aligning their content strategy with their unique voice and expertise, women build visibility, credibility, and influence. Their message is heard, recognised, and remembered - transforming knowledge into authority and creating lasting impact across multiple channels.

Diamond (Crown Chakra) – Brilliance: The Durable Partnerships Diamond™

This stage in the GemsCraft Journey represents the **tip of the diamond** - the visible brilliance built on all the work done in the previous steps (other "gems"). It focuses on **creating partnerships that are strong, reliable, and long-lasting,** turning your unique expertise and authority into enduring influence. It reflects not only stability but also the capacity of your network, collaborations, and alliances to withstand challenges while amplifying your impact over time.

Problem: Many women have developed their personal brand, content, and authority, yet struggle to translate this into **sustainable, high-value relationships.** Partnerships may be short-lived, opportunistic, or misaligned, limiting reach and impact.

Challenges:

- Identifying collaborators or partners who align with their values, vision, and unique offering.

- Sustaining relationships in competitive or fast-changing environments.

- Converting visibility and thought leadership into meaningful, long-term influence.

Consequences: Without durable partnerships, even highly capable women risk fragmented influence, missed opportunities, and diluted authority. Their expertise may be recognised in the short term but fail to generate lasting impact or legacy.

Solution: The Durable Partnerships Diamond™ guides women to strategically identify, build, and nurture collaborations that are aligned with their mission and strengths. It teaches how to transform connections into enduring alliances that amplify visibility, credibility, and influence. Women learn to operate at the tip of the diamond, where their accumulated work - skills, methodologies, and personal brand - shines most powerfully.

Advantage: By creating durable, high-value partnerships, women consolidate their authority, expand reach, and enhance long-term impact. These strategic collaborations magnify their value, inspire others, and ensure that their legacy endures, transforming individual brilliance into collective influence.

The Transformation: From Chasing to Attracting

The framework is a true journey of gem discovery and craftsmanship. I have experienced it myself, and I've seen it work for women in business. As you move through the process, you uncover and polish all seven gems, which together give you an integrated strategy.

When women complete this seven-gem journey, magic happens. They stop chasing clients and start attracting them. Internal alignment creates external magnetism. Confidence becomes unshakeable. Their story becomes their strategy, and premium positioning happens naturally.

When it comes to positioning your personal brand and standing out in the marketplace, you don't need to showcase all seven gems at once. This journey will help you **discover and focus on the few that shine brightest for you** - the ones most aligned with your true essence. By refining your energy and attention, your personal brand will become **clear, magnetic, and irresistibly authentic.**

Here are three transformational stories of women who discovered the Personal Brand Gems Framework and unlocked their unique brilliance.

Real Women, Real Transformations: The Gems Revealed

Indre's Transformation:

Indre, Wealth Coach, London & Milan.
When Indre first called me, her voice carried the weight of someone living a split life.

"I'm successful in banking, but I feel like I'm only addressing half of what women really need," she confessed. "I see them making smart financial investments while completely neglecting their health."

Her Ruby work revealed the hidden gem of her mother's wisdom, financial and physical health are inseparable. "What good is money in the bank if you're too sick to enjoy it?"

Her Carnelian spark came when she embraced her "crazy" idea of combining wealth coaching with wellness. What seemed impractical became her creative differentiator.

Her Citrine breakthrough arrived when she finally claimed her authority in this new integrated niche. She stepped into her power as a thought leader, pioneering a model that others now adopt.

Sara's Transformation:
Sara, London & Italy

"I'm whispering in a crowded room," Sara told me, describing her decade of feeling invisible despite transforming women's lives through style. Competing with Instagram-perfect stylists had nearly silenced her.

Her Emerald revelation was rediscovering her nonna's wisdom, style as quality, longevity, and care. This empathy-driven heritage became the foundation for her authentic connection with clients.

Her Sapphire turning point came when she found her voice. No longer whispering, she developed a confident, recognisable message becoming a Style Interpreter who communicates fashion as conscious life expression.

Marinella's Transformation:

Marinella, European Funds Consultant, Naples & Italy

"I feel trapped in this small box when I know I could be helping companies transform completely," Marinella admitted. Being labelled as "just a funding consultant" was suffocating.

Her Amethyst insight came when she realised her long-term vision, business was never just about funds but about guiding transformation with clarity and resilience.

Her Diamond moment was the integration of all her gems. She embraced her authentic brilliance as a Business Concierge, no longer boxed in, but recognised as a beacon, inspiring ambitious entrepreneurs. Today, she shines with influence, building legacy through her authentic worth.

The Thread That Connects: Pressure Creates Gems

Notice the pattern? Each woman's transformation didn't come from avoiding pressure, it came from understanding it as the force that reveals and polishes their authentic gems.

Most women never stop to discover their gems. They see only the rough stone. They forget the brilliance inside. This is why many lose themselves, buried beneath expectations, running in circles, polishing an image instead of uncovering their essence.

Indre's split between finance and wellness created the integration that revolutionised an industry. Sara's struggle with fast-fashion culture polished her into a sustainability pioneer.

Marinella's frustration with being "boxed in" shaped her into the Business Concierge, a role she now excels in.

And me? Sensitivity wasn't a weakness, it was a Ruby foundation. The so-called "crazy" ideas weren't flaws, they were Carnelian creativity. Together, they formed the Diamond brilliance waiting to shine. My own journey revealed how these hidden gems could be harnessed. Today, this insight shapes my work as a Human Personal Brand Creator, helping women uncover and polish their unique gems, transforming what makes them different into a personal brand that shines, resonates, and delivers tangible results, turning authenticity into influence, visibility, and business success.

Your Moment of Choice: The Gem Within You
Right now, as you read this, you stand at a crossroads. You can keep believing your sensitivity makes you weak, your creative ideas "crazy," your humanity unprofessional.

Or you can choose differently.

Every dismissal, every "you're too much," every "you're just crazy," every pressure you've carried has been shaping the precious gem that is authentically you.

The world doesn't need another manufactured personal brand. It needs your exact blend of sensitivity and strength, creativity and wisdom, humanity and authority. It needs the gem that only your unique pressures could create.

Being human makes you powerful. That teacher who tried to diminish my humanity? She unknowingly revealed my first gem, the Ruby of deep empathy and authentic connection.

Being "crazy" and creative makes you distinct. That partner who dismissed my ideas as nonsense? He applied the very pressure that shaped my Carnelian, purposeful, unapologetic innovation.

Every dismissal was actually discovery. Each crack revealed the raw materials that polished over time, became my authentic brand.

And here's the truth, *"in a marketplace of manufactured personas that profit from your insecurity, authenticity has become the rarest, and most valuable currency."*

The "Brilliance" Question.
The girl who felt too deeply. The woman with "wild" ideas. The professional who insisted humanity belongs in business. She wasn't broken, she was in formation, learning to carry the weight of her brilliance.

Your sensitivity. Your creativity. Your complexity. None of these are flaws. They are proof of your authenticity. The pressures you've endured haven't diminished you, they've been shaping you.

The world doesn't need another template brand. It needs you, your story, your essence, your worth. Don't let it stay hidden. So, I'll leave you with the question I ask every woman who begins this journey:

What if the qualities you've hidden to 'fit in' are raw, unpolished gems—the fire within you that can build a robust personal brand and transform lives?

The most precious things reveal their value only when they are brought into the light.

Your uniqueness awaits discovery. Your brilliance awaits expression. Your brand awaits creation, ready to shine.

Scan the QR code now to build a brand that shines like a diamond reflecting your worth and attracting the opportunities you deserve.

Marianna Penna

CEO & Founder, WOW Women of Worth London, PRCA London

Marianna Penna is the CEO & Founder of **WOW Women of Worth London,** Human Personal Brand Creator, Podcaster, Public Speaker, Event Organiser, and **G100 Italy Chair for Brand Creation & Marketing.** Born in Naples, Italy, with a degree in Economics, she has built a career across Italy and the UK, becoming a reference in authentic marketing and personal brand creation, helping women transform from invisible to irresistible, making them shine from the inside out.

Her career began in 2001 with major experience in finance as a controller for an American multinational in Italy, before moving into PR and marketing, managing international campaigns in food, fashion, and lifestyle. Later, as Marketing Director and Managing Partner at LEXeFISCAL LLP in London, she brought creativity and female leadership into the legal and fiscal sector.

In 2021, she founded WOW Women of Worth London to empower women entrepreneurs and professionals through a **holistic, human-centred marketing approach.** Her innovative frameworks guide women step by step: the **Marketing SPA concept** helps ground and balance their strategy; the **Natural Marketing Cycle Guide** translates this into an actionable roadmap; and the **Brand YOU GemsCraft Journey™** crystallises their unique identity into a distinctive, thriving personal brand.

Through WOW, her annual Marketing Festival "Walk The Talk" in London & Italy, her podcast Entrepreneurial Pulse, and live series WOW Voices Speak Volumes, and the last launched signature campaign and series of events promoting "AuthentiCITY" starting from the city of Naples in Italy, Marianna amplifies women's voices globally. With 25 years of international experience, she inspires women to align identity and business, creating brands that not only thrive, but leave legacies

Scan the QR code for More!

CHANGE
MAKERS
ENTREPRENEURS WITH A MISSION
VOICES WITH A MESSAGE
THE PROFESSIONAL SPEAKERS ACADEMY
UNLEASHING 17 VOICES, 17 JOURNEYS.
ONE RIPPLE EFFECT THAT WILL
TRANSFORM YOUR LIFE & BUSINESS.

CHAPTER 8

FREEDOM FORGED IN FIRE

HOW BETRAYAL, LOSS, AND PURPOSE BUILT MY PATH TO FREEDOM

Purpose turns
pain into power

- David Ravenscroft

It was the 28th of May 1999, and I was in my business partner George's office when he said,

"Hey Dave, you know that deal we've been discussing, the £10 million sale?"

"Yes," I replied.

"Well, we need to bring in a third party to help with the transaction. It'll take some time to close, but if you like, I'll buy your shares off you now, so you don't have to wait. How does that sound?"

"That's brilliant!" I said enthusiastically. "Thanks, mate. How will that work?"
"I'll get the lawyers to draw it up. It'll take a few weeks, and now we've agreed, you don't need to come into the office anymore. You'll still get paid and keep your Lotus Esprit Turbo company car until everything's signed."

"Ok mate, nice one."

We shook hands, and I walked out, relieved and optimistic.

Betrayal

The summer of '99 rolled on, but weeks dragged into months as the lawyers disappeared on holiday.

By Sunday, 29th August, I was in Tunisia at the Marhaba Palace Hotel, sat at the pool bar after a day at the beach. I'd just ordered a Tibérine and Coke, a local liqueur that goes down far too easily.

I picked up the phone to nudge George about the deal and to check on my dividend payment. Three months had passed, and things were dragging.

Changemakers

"Hiya George, are we any nearer to getting the deal done?" I asked.
"I'm working on it, Dave," he said.

"Ok mate, how about some dividends?"

"We don't have the spare funds at the moment."

"Oh… I thought you'd just bought another Ferrari?" I asked.

"Don't get f***ing clever, Dave!" he snapped.

"I'm not being clever, George, I'm only asking for what I'm due."
"That's it!" he shouted and hung up.

The next morning, I flew home. Waiting for me was a letter from HR. "You've been summarily dismissed for gross misconduct. Your salary and phone will be terminated. Your car and laptop will be picked up on Friday 3rd September."

I was in shock. George wasn't just a partner; he was someone I trusted like a brother. I had poured seven years of hard work into that company. When I joined, they were turning over a few hundred thousand and keeping records on 6x9 index cards. I computerised the systems, built processes, and helped push us toward £10 million in revenue. But in all of it, I'd neglected my own protection.

The news spread locally like wildfire. Some people relished my downfall. "You f***ed up there, didn't you?" one sneered.

"He's f***ed up," I shot back.

"Well, it doesn't look like it from where I'm sitting!" came the retort. And I couldn't argue with that.

The reasons for my dismissal were manufactured, the most ridiculous being that I hadn't been in the office for three months, though George himself had told me not to come in.

I went to see a lawyer. With no share certificates, no contract of employment, and no shareholder agreement, my only chance was an unfair dismissal claim. It was going to be long, expensive, and draining. So, I sought advice from a friend, the CEO of a PLC. After hearing me out, he said,

"Dave, you're not the first person to get kicked out of a company you helped build, and you won't be the last. Why don't you set up again, but do it right this time? Get your shareholders' agreements and contracts in place."

That advice was the turning point.

Starting Again

I set up a new company with three partners. The first two years were tough, still battling George's lawyers. On the day of the court hearing, they called with offers. At first it was insulting, my old car and a Rolex. I told them exactly where they could shove it.

Thirty minutes before court, I accepted a six-figure cash settlement. Nowhere near the £10 million once on the table, but it gave me closure and space to start fresh.

Within twelve months, we'd landed a major contract worth millions. Soon after, Australia Post signed on, and suddenly, we were international. By 2007, the company was flying. My partners and I stepped back from day-to-day operations. We still owned the business, but we now had time and financial freedom.

I became an offshore yacht master, bought a penthouse in Mallorca, and a yacht. I invested in property, renovated homes, and even bought my mum a house.

Life was good.

Cayman Life & Shakara

By 2010, with tax hikes in the UK, I moved to the Cayman Islands. Sunshine, health, freedom, I was living the dream.

I met Shakara in late 2009, and she joined me in Cayman. She was the love of my life. We built a beautiful future together.

But on 30th May 2013, tragedy struck. A call came from the Cayman police,

"Do you have a white pickup truck?"

"Yes."

"Was your fiancée driving it?"

"Yes, has she had an accident?"

"She's been involved in an incident. She's dead."

My world collapsed in that moment. The woman I loved was gone.

The days that followed were a blur. Friends and family supported me, but grief was overwhelming. My mate Steve, who'd lost his own wife, said, "I threw myself into work, Dave."

So that's what I did.

Rebuilding

I grew my UK property portfolio, launched a lettings agency, and invested heavily. I travelled the world, searching for meaning.

In Thailand, I met Gift, who helped me settle in. Through her, I met someone special, and love found me again when I least expected it.

In 2015, problems arose in Australia with our marketing company. A failed software rollout nearly destroyed us. We faced either shutting down or risking a $20 million fine. I came out of retirement to fix it. Within twelve months, we negotiated with the ACCC, paid a six-figure fine, and sold the Australian division for an eight-figure payout.

By 2016, I had seen the pattern clearly: partnerships, purpose, systems, and resilience.

The Blueprint

Every chapter of my life, success, betrayal, loss, rebuilding, taught me the same truth: business freedom isn't about the money. It's about building value, having systems, choosing the right people, and being prepared.

That's why I created The Business Freedom Blueprint, a framework to help entrepreneurs design businesses that run smoothly, scale effectively, and are always sale-ready.

Because if there's one thing I know for sure, it's this, freedom isn't given, it's built.

The reason I've shared these stories is there's a theme that runs through my life. All my businesses have been with partners. There has always been a purpose to my life and that is still true today. I love nothing more than working with purpose driven business owners and entrepreneurs, helping and guiding them to create value in their businesses by hiring the right people and putting the correct systems and process in place. This increases the value of their business and makes it sale ready at any time, so they have the opportunity to fulfil their destiny.

That's why I developed The Business Freedom Blueprint.

The Business *Freedom* Blueprint…

Business *Freedom* Hub.com™

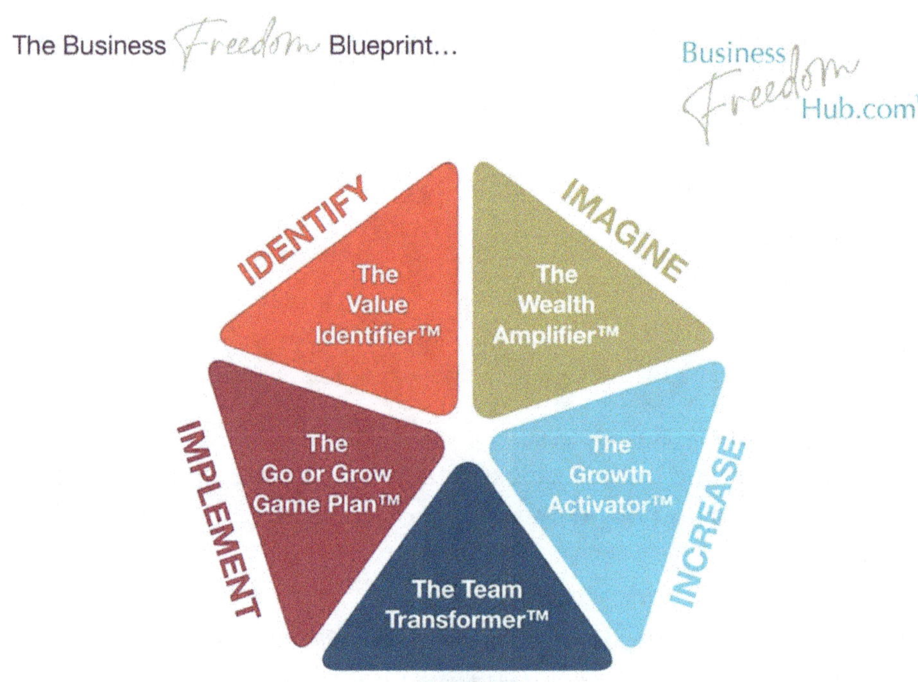

Here's a picture of The Business Freedom Blueprint.

1. IDENTIFY – The Value Identifier

The first step is to identify the true value of your business not the figure in your head, but what an investor or buyer would pay today.

Most owners don't know that number. They confuse revenue with value, or assume profit multiples will apply directly. But years of tax-minimisation strategies and personal expenses through the business often make accounts look weak, even if the business is strong.

The result? Disappointment at the negotiating table, false expectations, and deals that fall apart.
Even when sales happen, they often come with long "earn-outs" to justify a higher price keeping owners tied to a business they thought they'd left behind.

That's why the Blueprint begins with the Value Identifier. By stripping away noise and calculating true EBITDA, then understanding how multiples apply, business owners see clarity and opportunity.
This is the foundation: knowing what the business is really worth, and what it could be worth.

2. IMAGINE – The Wealth Amplifier

The second pillar is Imagine, building a compelling personal and financial vision for life after business.

Many owners think they're ready to sell, until they face the reality of life without their "money-making machine." Doubts creep in: Do I really have enough? Partners or family members raise late-stage concerns, sometimes halting deals entirely.

The net effect of not preparing personally is hesitation, regret, or underselling. Instead of freedom, owners risk ongoing uncertainty and even stepping back into the business they wanted to leave.

The Wealth Amplifier fixes this. Through structured questions, analysis, and planning, business owners map out exactly what they'll need, income, lump sums, lifestyle goals. The result is clarity in black and white, giving confidence to proceed when the right offer arrives.

3. INCREASE – The Growth Activator

The third pillar is Increase, activating smart, sustainable growth that drives value higher.

Flatlining businesses quickly lose their appeal. Buyers want to see momentum, systems, and
structure. Yet many owners chase short-term profit rather than building long-term stability.

The outcome is often chaos: over-reliance on one major client, weak margins, or growth that makes the business harder, not easier, to run. Value is capped or even reduced.

The Growth Activator reverses this. By professionalising operations, strengthening systems, and diversifying revenue, the business becomes more scalable, more resilient, and far more attractive to buyers.

4. INVITE – The Team Transformer

The fourth pillar is Invite, bringing in the right external professionals. Not operational staff, but advisors who protect the business and position it for sale.

The mistake? Relying on an end-of-year accountant who's never seen an M&A deal. Or trusting an online broker promising free valuations. Or, worse, having professionals who never coordinate, leaving the owner lost between conflicting advice.

This leads to false expectations, wasted time, collapsed deals, or exposure to risk from poor structuring and lack of protection.

With the Team Transformer, owners surround themselves with the right accountant, lawyer, tax expert, financial advisor, and broker or banker (when needed), all aligned and working together. The business is now operating at a professional level, with a team ready to act when the moment comes.

5. IMPLEMENT – The Go or Grow Game Plan

The final pillar is Implement. This is where strategy becomes execution, using the Go or Grow Game Plan. Every 90 days, the business owner and their advisor decide, grow the business further, or prepare it for sale.

Most owners drift. They chase sales, mistake activity for progress, or try to "fix everything" at once. Instead of clarity, they create a bigger, riskier version of the same problems.

The effect? Growth feels like firefighting and exit becomes rushed and reactive. They sell for less, or stay trapped for longer.

With the Go or Grow Game Plan, every quarter has focus. If the goal is growth, the focus is on strengthening systems, diversifying revenue, or professionalising operations. If the goal is sale, the focus shifts to tightening costs, protecting profits, and crucially identifying but not acting on future opportunities, so they can be presented to the buyer as upside. Either way, the business owner stays in control, compounding value while always being ready.

Because, in the end, it's not the businesses we build or the deals we close that define us, it's the purpose that drives us forward, giving meaning to everything we create and legacy that outlives us.

Never lose sight of your purpose!

What's Next?

If you're a business owner who wants to make your company more valuable and achieve true business freedom, I've created a presentation specifically for you.

Simply scan the QR code below, and you'll be taken straight to a page where you can watch it immediately.

And here's the best part, if what you see resonates, and you'd like to explore working with me personally, there's a link at the end of that presentation where you can complete a short questionnaire. From there, if it looks like a good fit for both of us, we can arrange a private conversation about your business.

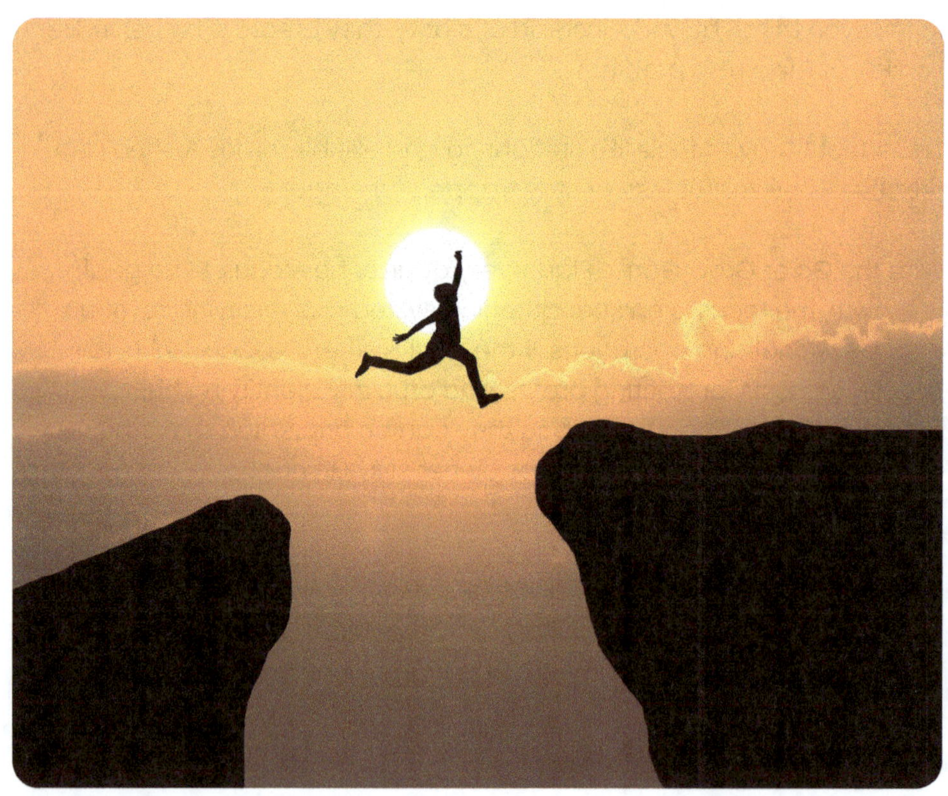

David Ravenscroft is a serial entrepreneur and has spent more than 40 years building businesses across five continents learning firsthand the highs, lows, and life-changing lessons of entrepreneurship. Over the years, he has successfully exited companies three times, with deals ranging from six to eight figures. But ask him what he's most proud of, and he'll tell you it's not the numbers, it's the people, the adventures, and the purpose behind it all.

From boardrooms to building sites, courtrooms to tropical coastlines, David has always followed his instinct for opportunity and his belief that business should create freedom not stress. Today, that freedom looks like life in Thailand with his wife and two children, where he continues investing in and supporting entrepreneurs who want their business to serve their life, not consume it.

At his core, David is driven by one thing: helping purpose-driven founders build businesses they can one day step back from knowing they've created something that truly matters.

I'd love you to take that step. Here's the QR code I hope that I get to meet you.

CHANGE
MAKERS
ENTREPRENEURS WITH A MISSION
VOICES WITH A MESSAGE
THE PROFESSIONAL SPEAKERS ACADEMY
UNLEASHING 17 VOICES, 17 JOURNEYS.
ONE RIPPLE EFFECT THAT WILL
TRANSFORM YOUR LIFE & BUSINESS.

CHAPTER 9
LIFE LESSONS FROM THE BIG C

"It's when we are challenged,
that we truly discover our inner
strength."

- Kevin Wright

• • •

"Mr Wright, you have a big problem. You have Non-Hodgkin's Lymphoma"
With those words, my consultant delivered the diagnosis that I had cancer.
Cancer, just the word sends shivers down your spine, doesn't it?
According to Cancer Research UK, the statistics for survival for all
non-Hodgkin lymphomas (NHL) in England are:

- Around 80 out of every 100 people (around 80%) survive their cancer
  for 1 year or more after they are diagnosed.

- Around 65 out of every 100 people (around 65%) survive their cancer
  for 5 years or more after diagnosis.

- It is predicted that 55 out of every 100 people (55%) will survive their
  cancer for 10 years or more after they are diagnosed.

Looking at this from the outside, this sounds hopeful, but when you are
diagnosed, you are likely to have a very different viewpoint. Nobody wants
to be in the 45% that don't survive for 10 years after diagnosis. I determined
that I would be in the survivors, or better still conquerors category.

Why is this important?

This is not just about dealing with cancer, but how to manage your
mind-set to achieve whatever you decide you want.

I've applied it to my business as well as my personal life, and I teach my
property Ninjas Investors (mentees) how to harness a millionaire mindset to achieve their portfolio building goals.

I set about applying the same techniques to dealing with my diagnosis.
I call this approach:

The V.I.T.A.L. Conqueror Blueprint

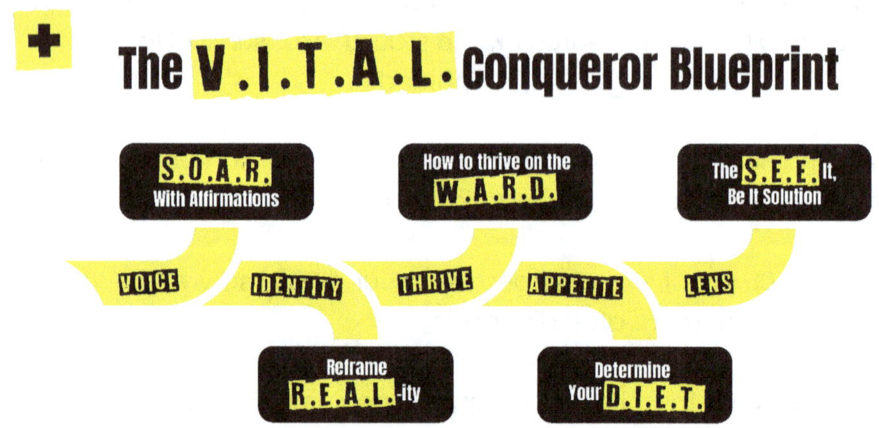

From my early thirties, I developed a thirst for knowledge about personal development, acquiring a library of self-development books. These formulated beliefs underpin the way I prepare for, react to and live life in general.

When it came to dealing with my diagnosis, I determined this was going to be a three-pronged attack :

The mental approach – using the power of my mind.

The research approach – learning as much as I could so my decisions were informed.

The medical approach – chemotherapy.

For decades, people, just ordinary people like me, have been using the infinite power of their mind, often unwittingly, to help heal their body of a variety of ailments.

V – Voice

I've actively practised Neuro Linguistic Programming (NLP) since the late 1990s, working with an NLP Master Practitioner. While I continue to use this skill informally, my diagnosis meant that I knew I was going to need support to keep my mind-set on track.

NLP taught me that I have the ability to re-frame any circumstance, any situation and determine my own meaning to it.

I looked for a local NLP Master Practitioner and having found one I felt was a good fit, we set about installing affirmations and creating visualisations.

If you're thinking 'but I don't have that health situation to deal with, so what has this to do with me?' These techniques can be applied to any challenge you want to overcome.

The first step for me was to install the right mindset and teach my internal voice to run the positive affirmations that would help me achieve a positive outcome.

I reasoned that allowing myself to think negative thoughts was detrimental to my mental state. If you believe that what goes on in your mind can greatly influence what goes on in your body, then each negative thought I allowed myself to have would be harming my body, and my body needed all the help my mind could possibly give it.

Not just thoughts though, words too, dialogue both internal and external. To get the best result, I had to be the guardian of both thoughts and words, and sentry duty was a 24 hour a day responsibility.

I discovered a quote some years ago that greatly helped me to position how to organise and control my thoughts and the grave risks of not doing so.

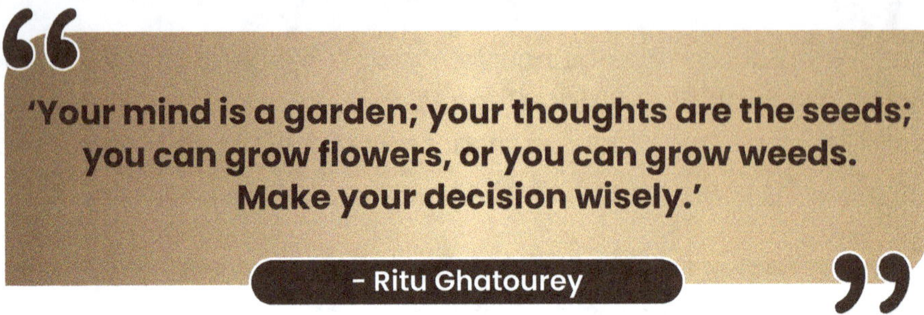

Weeds equal negative thoughts and words, and flowers (positive intentions, thoughts and deeds) are the positive counterbalance. In a garden left unattended, naturally weeds will grow, no effort is required. For flowers to grow and flourish in a garden, it takes both time and effort.

The great news here is that the conscious mind cannot hold both a negative and positive thought simultaneously. Knowing that means that we can knowingly block out a negative thought with a positive one. This takes some practice, but it does get easier the more we do it.

I determined, almost from diagnosis, to introduce a phrase into my daily life...

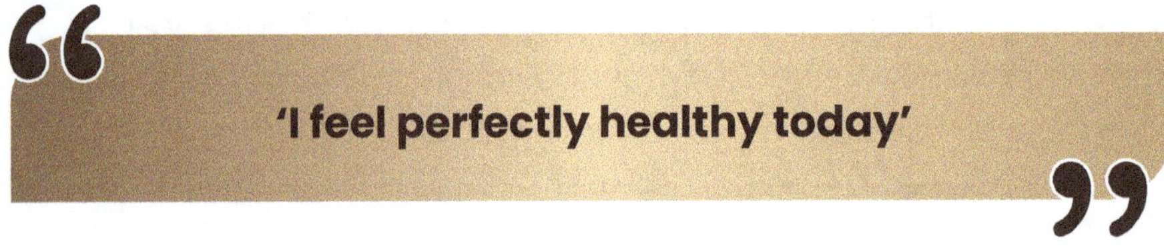

My intention being to use it as an affirmation, dropped into as many conversations as I can, both written and verbal as well as internally to myself. This was the precise message I wanted to send to my unconscious mind.

Some years previously I found this old Native American Cherokee legend, told through the generations of The Two Wolves.

An old Cherokee is teaching his grandson about life. "A fight is going on inside me" he said to the boy.

> *"It is a terrible fight, and it is between two wolves. One is evil – he is anger, envy, sorrow, regret, greed, arrogance, self-pity, guilt, resentment, inferiority, lies, false pride, superiority and ego."*

> *He continued "The other is good – he is joy, peace, love, hope, serenity, humility, kindness, benevolence, empathy, generosity, truth, compassion and faith. The same fight is going on inside you – and inside every other person too."*

> *The grandson thought about this for a minute and then asked his grandfather "Which wolf will win?"*

> *The old Cherokee simply replied "The one you feed"*

I found a simplicity and honesty in this that had a profound effect on the way I was determined to think in the future. It was a no-brainer to resolve that my evil wolf would die of starvation; I would feed my good wolf until he was full, every day.

We chatter to ourselves continually, usually internally, it's that voice in your head that you hold entire conversations with. Unfortunately, left to its own devices, that chatter can be completely negative which is the last thing you need when you are experiencing cancer – or facing any other challenge.

When I'm working with people who are looking at either starting out in property, or taking a leap to bigger and more profitable deals, there's a lot of this negative internal chatter going on in their heads,

"Everyone knows that property investing is risky, I could lose my savings."

"How will I know which deals are good and which are going to wipe me out?"

Changemakers

"It's a big step, maybe I should be satisfied with the way things are."

Whether it's property investment or any other career, the same kind of negative thoughts echo through our minds. There's a risk, and fear can have two effects, it will either persuade you to play safe and not take action, or it will give you the adrenaline to take BIG action and do everything you can think of to ensure you succeed. Your internal conversations need to be trained to help rather than hinder.

Your unconscious mind is mostly unjudgmental, whatever we believe or tell ourselves, it will accept as our truth. It doesn't matter if these thoughts are negative or positive, the unconscious will accept either. Human beings have absolute control over the material that reaches their unconscious mind through the five senses, although few regularly exercise this control.

The human brain is an incredibly powerful personal computer that is capable of providing the power to achieve your goals, if you treat it in the right way to gain the most benefit.

Your friends, family and business colleagues may not share your beliefs, and almost certainly, someone will try to persuade you that this course of action is not for you.

The secret is persistence, repetition and determination.

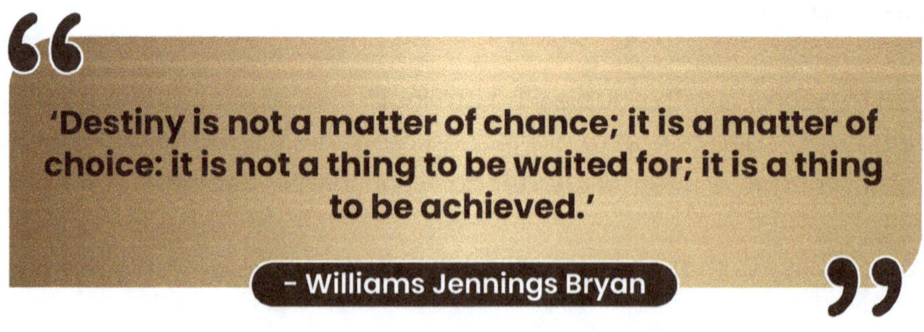

I – Identity

One of the ten NLP presuppositions is,

'The map is not the territory'

In other words, we interpret the world, not as it is in reality, but how we see it based on our own belief systems. We generalise, delete and distort true reality to fit how we perceive things to be, our view of the world. For example, two unconnected people attend the same party. One found it a drab affair, the people were unfriendly, he spoke to almost no-one, hung around in the kitchen and left early. The other said that it was a fantastic party, the people were great, he made some new friends, he drank and danced and was one of the last to leave. It was the same party, but these two people experienced it completely differently.

Cognitive Reframing is understanding that how I see the world is my own free choice. My reframe in this case was to view my cancer diagnosis as that reframe fundamentally changed the way I reacted to the whole experience I had ahead of me.

> **'A wonderful opportunity to conduct a real-life experiment to find out to what degree I can use my mind to control what happens in my body'**

This applies to any challenge you may be facing. You choose how you perceive it.

Reframing provides the means to take any given situation or experience, and by placing a different frame around it, change its meaning, either directly or by placing it in an alternative context in which it means something else.

Changemakers

As Eleanor Roosevelt once pointed out,

"No-one can insult you unless you choose to be insulted."

You have a choice in how you respond to events in your life. If there is one thing in life no one else can control, it's our thoughts, we have the power to choose these.

Meaning influences behaviour. Change the meaning and you can modify your behaviour, so you respond in different ways.

Someone new to this form of thinking may find this to be a tall order but, although I have the advantage of years of familiarisation, that doesn't mean that someone new to this framework cannot understand and implement this thought process. My advice is to find an NLP Master Practitioner in your locality to help you become more effective.

Asking better questions is a method often used to elicit a different thought process. A simple example is the difference between the thoughts:

1.   'I can't do this'

2.   'I don't think I can do this'

3.   'How can I do this?'

The first is a statement of your negative belief, a certainty. The second is less negative but displays uncertainty. The third is a search for the answer and it also engages the help of the unconscious mind to find the solution, and it will.

T – Thrive

Letting things happen to you is not a good recipe for success in any field or situation. To succeed you need to take charge of your situation. Personally facing a serious health challenge meant finding out about the medical process, what to expect, what was expected of me and where there was room for me to push the parameters beyond those expectations.

To thrive I needed to be well-informed, but not just to accept that everything must follow other people's expectations. I'm not talking about rocking the boat and being difficult, after all, I needed the medical people on my side, but I'm referring to where I could apply my own approach.

This turned chemo treatments into a double-edged sword. The chemicals attacked the cancer cells, while at the same time I was using visualisation and meditation to mentally zap the cells, watching them die and shrivel away.

Everyone else in the chemo treatment room was reading, watching TV or scrolling on their phones. In fact, most of the nurses just assumed I was asleep, but I was mentally active internally to ensure my body thrived. Regardless of the situation in which you find yourself, it's important to understand all the elements before you start taking steps to shape things to how you want them to be.

A – Appetite

I was surprised to discover that the consultant had very little advice about diet, so I set about finding out about what might help me to combat those pesky cancer cells.

My first decision was to eliminate sugar. The PET scan used glucose to make the cancer cells active and visible. I definitely didn't want to feed them that. But then I looked into what else I could do and found an excellent book, listing the foods to avoid and, better still, what I could add to my diet.

This wasn't a weight reduction diet; it was a life affirming eating plan. I did drop a few pounds, but the main focus was to feed my system with the foods that would make my body a more difficult environment for cancer to thrive in.

This strategy fed my appetite for health. If you're not fighting a health condition, you may wonder what this has to do with achieving your goals. In my view, it's simple. You need to be fit for the future – that's the future you're choosing.

Whether you need to eat better, exercise more, or get more replenishing sleep, if you don't look after yourself, you won't have the reserves to take those essential steps forward.

It was interesting to note that while everyone was warning me of the dramatic energy drain chemo would have, I never experienced these. In fact, in the days following my chemo treatment I found I was more alert than usual and actually needed fewer hours of sleep.

I haven't researched the impact of an alkaline diet on energy levels, but the major change to my diet and mental approach definitely kept me in good shape while I fought the condition.

L – Lens

When we are in a mindset of fear, we inevitably create 'disaster movies' in our heads, the last thing we need to be doing when dealing with a cancer diagnosis. It is much better to create 'happy ending' movies. You choose the lens through which you view your situation.

Visualisation is one of the most powerful mindset techniques at our disposal. Elite athletes have used this technique in recent decades, creating very powerful visualisations of positive outcomes that they program into their unconscious minds.

We experience bodily changes when out of our comfort zone, shallower breathing, faster heartrate, sweatier palms, all classic 'fight or flight' responses. We exhibit these when it's a real-life situation, but also when we are just imagining doing something we are not comfortable with or have never done before.

The unconscious mind can misinterpret these feelings as a threat, remember its primary purpose is our survival. When we are imagining something out of our comfort zone or experience, displaying those 'fight or flight' symptoms, it's easy for the unconscious mind to trigger negative outcomes in an attempt to get us back in our comfort zone. It is not serving us to create the results we want. The resolution to this is to use our conscious mind to override negative images and create the positive outcomes we want.

You are in charge of your future.

Within NLP, Modelling is the process of recreating excellence. If one person can do something, it is possible to model it and teach it to others. In this way everyone can learn to get better results in their own way.

What you have read so far can be a template, the model that you copy to achieve your own result. But let's look at probably one of the best-known examples of modelling. People don't generally think of it as modelling, but, when you drill down a bit deeper, that's exactly what it is.

It was on 6th May 1954 that Roger Bannister became the first man in history to run a mile in under four minutes. Decades later, the momentousness of such an achievement is probably dimmed somewhat, but, back then, it was big. In fact, it was bigger than big; it was HUGE.

The world record for the mile back then had been stuck at 4:01:4 for some time. Medical opinion was divided on whether it was physically possible for man to run a mile in under four minutes.

> *John Landy, an Australian and competitor of Bannister in the previous Olympic Games, was the poster boy of the time, pushing himself closer to the magic four-minute mile. But he was quoted as saying "The four-minute mile is a brick wall, and I shan't attempt it again."*
>
> *Then something happened. Medical student, Roger Bannister, took to the Iffley Road track in Oxford, on 6th May 1954, and ran 3:59:4.*
>
> *The barrier is conquered, the wall was broken, and lo-and-behold, John Landy, the man who failed six times, ran 3:58.0 six weeks later!*
>
> *From then more and more athletes achieved the 'impossible', they ran a mile in under four minutes.*
>
> *How did Landy suddenly mirror what Bannister achieved only weeks later when previously he had continually come up short? He changed his process, he modelled Bannister, he copied what Bannister did using pacesetters, having previously run alone. When Landy eventually broke four minutes with his 3.58, he not only had pacesetters, but competitors who pushed him all the way through to the bell.*
>
> *He also changed location, to Finland, where they had better quality track surfaces, similar to those Bannister used in England.*

The real point is that if someone else has proved it's possible, 'impossible' is no longer a valid reason.

Become your own film director.

Make your own mind movies visualising success, make them engaging, make them empowering, and make them triumphant. Get clarity on what the best result you could have is, then create your movie around that. What would it look, sound, smell, and feel like? Use those sub-modalities we learned earlier to make it compelling.

And replay it constantly, many times daily. Tweak it, edit it if you uncover ways to make it even more empowering.

Strategies for success

Manage your attitude

A positive attitude is not an act; it must be genuine. When things are going well, a positive attitude becomes self-perpetuating and easy to maintain.

Changemakers

It doesn't matter how many times you fall down. It's the number of times that you get back up that counts.

Henry Ford is credited with this gem of wisdom, but there is a much older Japanese proverb that states this:

'Fall down 7 times, get up 8'

A positive attitude is a state of mind which can be maintained only through conscious effort.

Train your mind

The unconscious is trainable; you train it with certain thoughts and principles and beliefs. Once these are set in your mind it becomes difficult to change them – but not impossible. While you try and change a habit you've learned, your unconscious is constantly resisting. The only way to beat it is to keep persisting until it believes in the new idea/course. Once it has belief and faith in that route it will start protecting the new path and follow it just as fervently as the original route.
With this in mind you can understand why we all have great ideas, even make promises (New Year's resolutions) to ourselves and somehow never follow them through.

The unconscious mind is very clever when it stops us, it not only tells us to stop, but it also comes up with lots of rational reasons why we should maintain the existing situation. You've probably had conversations with yourself in these situations.

'Eating salads in January isn't good, the produce isn't as good quality as in the summer and my body needs fuel to combat the cold temperatures.'

'Going for a run in the dark is dangerous, it would be better to wait until the mornings/evenings are lighter.'

'It isn't a good time to start prospecting for new clients, I'll wait until the beginning of the new financial year, when people have the budget to spend.'

Remember when you are rationalising you are telling yourself Rational Lies.

'Faced with the choice between changing one's mind and proving there is no need to do so, almost everyone gets busy on the proof.'

– John Kenneth Galbraith

Listen to your internal voice and argue back when it starts coming up with negative language. Reposition that thought in a positive way and keep doing that until the new way becomes a habit.

It takes approximately 30 days to change a habit or route. Don't give up; if you persist you can achieve anything.

So, what's your big challenge?
What can you do to help your mindset focus on success?

The next step

If you or someone you care about would like to dig deeper into my strategies for conquering cancer, I've written a not-for-profit book and created an equally not-for-profit video programme that details my V.I.T.A.L. Conqueror Blueprint approach. You can find out more about both here: www.thinkpositivelyaboutcancer.com

If the above isn't you at this time but you'd like to explore the Millionaire Mindset, there is a video programme exploring how to apply this here: www.recycleyourcash.co.uk/store

Postscript: If you're wondering how my strategies worked in relation to my health. I had fewer chemo treatments than originally prescribed, my second PET scan showed a 99% reduction in cancer cells, and I had virtually no symptoms or after-effects from the chemo, other than some hair loss. I continued to work as normal throughout. I proved these techniques work, not just for health, but in my business too.

Kevin Wright is a property trainer with a difference – he doesn't just teach what to do, but shows people how to do it, step-by-step. He also encourages his delegates to adopt a millionaire mindset to help them achieve their goals.

He runs regular training sessions including online workshops, 1 and 3-day experiences as well as his in-depth Ninja Investor Programme and both a mentoring programme and a mastermind group. He has established one of the fastest growing property networks in the UK - Recycle Your Cash Property Chats. This is different from any other property networking group, no fees, no speakers and no BS, just pure property networking.

Scan the QR code for More!

CHANGE MAKERS

ENTREPRENEURS WITH A MISSION
VOICES WITH A MESSAGE

THE PROFESSIONAL SPEAKERS ACADEMY
UNLEASHING 17 VOICES, 17 JOURNEYS.

ONE RIPPLE EFFECT THAT WILL TRANSFORM YOUR LIFE & BUSINESS.

CHAPTER 10

MOVES OF THE INFINITE PLAYER IN THIS GAME CALLED LIFE

"

"A belief is a thought that you continue to think, and your thoughts are the mental architects that create your future, choose them both wisely."

- Donna Marie Costello

• • •

"

It's Monday October 17th, 2022, 3.30am and I am rudely awakened by the harsh siren sound of my alarm. As I walk half asleep to my bathroom to commence my morning routine, I gaze in the mirror and think to myself "there has to be more to life than this." The ungratefulness of a secure position as the Director of a fencing retail yard, within a long-standing established family fencing erection business was starting to overwhelm me.

I was starting to feel like my days were equivalent to a wild animal caged up for the purpose of human entertainment, albeit I was trapped in a portal cabin for 12-14 hours per day, 5 days per week. Every day was Groundhog day, arise early, go to work, come home, microwave meal and bed.

However, little did I know that today was going to be the day that I experience a spiritual awakening.

As I arrive at work and get out of my car, I feel a chill as the cool autumnal breeze flows through me. First things first "a coffee" to warm up the cockles and awaken my senses, I say to myself.

6am and our first customer arrives. I greet him with a smile, and we exchange pleasantries, I ask him if he had a good weekend and he proceeds to tell me all about it. It certainly sounded fun filled as I listened with a look of enthusiasm, but deep down inside, I was feeling resentful. I think back to the days when I looked forward to Friday night's as they always kickstarted the weekends social gatherings.

However, over the past couple of years I had been declining social invitations as the long hours during the week were taking their toll on me. I much preferred to stay in and relax with a movie. A far cry from the social butterfly that I used to be.

With my customer's order placed, I take payment and he departs out into the yard to have his van loaded.

As I return to my desk and sit down to enjoy a now lukewarm mug of coffee, a voice arose inside of me, a voice that was gentle yet meaningful saying "it's time to go,
it's time to leave".

I have always had a strong intuition but my experience of it has always been a feeling rather than the voice that I just heard. I sat with it for a moment, but shortly after, I heard it again as clear as day, and this time the voice was stronger "it is time to go, it is time to leave".

My first reaction to it was to question "but what will I do?" then I thought to myself "I haven't been happy in a long time." Over the past 14 years I had successfully achieved getting the next division of the company off the ground even when at first it appeared the odds were stacked against me. I was a woman in a man's world and had little knowledge about fencing. However, I successfully secured our place on the map alongside the 2 main long standing fencing retailers within 3 years. Throughout the next 11 years the business continued to soar, but my passion had diminished. My intuition was right; it was time to leave. For ease of tying everything up in the business, I set my departure date for the 30th of June 2023, to allow my departure to coincide with the end of the financial year.

Once I had spoken my decision out loud, I knew for sure I had made the right one as an overwhelming sense of peace rose up within me. It was like the lioness was set free from her cage to roam free in the wilderness.

A couple of months prior to leaving I still hadn't decided what the "right next move" was. I knew a definite change was required. I wanted to experience a new enthusiasm for life. I wanted to find a career that I was passionate about. I wanted to wake up every morning with a spring in my step grateful for the opportunity to experience another great day. With these desires in mind, I stepped out of my comfort zone and invested in myself for the first time ever with a spiritual mentor to teach me personal development and growth.

Investing in myself was the greatest decision I have ever made. Learning about the truth of this universe, its energy, the gifts we hold inside and how to work in harmony with universal laws completely changed my life, but more importantly understanding my soul's purpose and elevating my consciousness completely transformed me as a person.

From my early 20's I suffered with anxiety, a state that I learnt to hide from the outside world. The feeling of unease within my body was a daily occurrence, brought on by an underlying programme in my subconscious mind that I was not good enough where friendships or romantic relationships were concerned. A lack of self-worth conditioned me to have the disease to please, to overcompensate the emotions I was feeling, but this often led to the being betrayed by others or being taken advantage of.

My personal life appeared to be a never-ending ride on a merry-go-round, the same situations kept arising just with different people playing different characters.

My pity parties were starting to become more frequent as I sat and thought to myself, "why does life keep throwing me curve balls when all I do is try to do my best for others?"

The answer was made clear to me; we are all spiritual beings having a human existence, and these were beliefs within my consciousness and an opportunity to expand my soul. The scenarios that I experienced were an opportunity to eradicate my soul's baggage and heal from the belief's that I was unworthy, that I needed validation from others to make me feel whole and that love was attained from the outside.

In order for my soul to correct these beliefs, I had to change my perspective and look at the challenges as an opportunity for my soul to grow. Understanding that lasting change can only come from transforming my internal state from feeling unworthy to worthy, the need for validation to an understanding that I am already whole, and the need to seek love from external things to love myself first and then love others without fear.

Through the correction of my soul, I could feel my connection to source energy strengthen, my intuition was getting a lot stronger, and a sense of protection surrounded me. I was also elevating my consciousness to new levels of awareness, and this gave the experiences a new sense of purpose. Every time I responded to life instead of reacting to it, I was filling my cup of wholeness up and gaining credits towards this game of life.

Consciousness is the one and only creator, and I kept recreating the same scenarios in my personal life because I was creating from my memories, whereas in business, my consciousness was focused on a vision.

Understanding that life is just a mirror to our thoughts, memories, feelings, and beliefs, and these things are what makes up our consciousness, made it easy to comprehend why I was successful in my career and unsuccessful in my personal life.

However, I am pleased to say that the corrections I have made with my consciousness using the tools given to me by my mentor have accelerated my experiences in life in a way that I can only describe as magical. In the past year, I have manifested the love of my life, a new home in a new county, a book deal and the opportunity to be a participant and tell my story alongside other powerful change makers within this book.

In relation to my body, expanding my soul and my consciousness to understand the truth of this universe and the truth of who I am, resulted in the anxiety to completely dissolve. For the first time in 30 years, my emotional state is one filled with peace and tranquillity.

As for my career, well that was easy, I was so inspired by the wisdom that I had embodied that changed my life, I decided to become a spiritual mentor and help others to heal their souls and elevate their consciousness. My niche is one with business owners, entrepreneurs, sole traders and managers.

We have all been taught that to be successful, you have to hustle and grind, and yes working the hours I did, I believed that too. However, there is an easier way, the effortless way and that is breaking away from the ego and working from the soul's perspective in conjunction with source energy.

Changemakers

Through my programmes I firstly…

EDUCATE my clients on the truth of who they are, how the universe operates, and bring awareness to the universal laws. I shed light on the universal energy and the importance of aligning with this energy. I also incorporate the teachings of our inner sight, mindfulness and the importance of having an empowered identity.

ELIMINATE the release of all negative self-talk, old beliefs, any guilt & shame, perfectionism, the past, comparison to others, the need for approval and judgement towards themselves and others.

ENVISAGE creating the right consciousness, how to use the imagination correctly, the power of meditation, the embodiment of this material in contrast to just gaining knowledge, the importance of aligning thoughts, feelings, beliefs and actions. Acting from the place that your desires have already been received and feeling the feelings of gratitude for them in the present moment are all necessary attributes to manifesting a life by design.

EXCHANGE all old patterns for the creation of new habits, beliefs, attitude, behaviours, assumptions, self-love and a new lifestyle.

ENHANCE the importance of having a spiritual practice to keep you connected to source energy for the continued expansion of your soul, together with self growth, self-talk, self-belief, self-discipline, self-approval and self-responsibility.

ELEVATE, now it is time to transform as you will have complete certainty. Knowing that you are limitless, that your level of awareness is now elevated, you will recognise guidance from source energy through your intuition, you will radiate a new profound confidence that will be an authentic version of yourself that is a magnet for miracles.

It is Monday 8th September 2025, it's 3.30am... and I am sound asleep! Long gone are the days that I am rudely awakened by the harsh siren sound of my alarm to signify another 12-14-hour day in a portal cabin.

Instead, I rise at 5am with a spring in my step grateful for the opportunity to experience another great day, one filled with enthusiasm for my new life and passion for the opportunity to assist other beautiful souls with their own transformations.

I chuckle to myself as a thought enters my mind, "Life is just a game".

Are you ready to play?

Donna Marie Costello is a passionate spiritual mentor for entrepreneurs, business owners and managers seeking to unlock their fullest potential through the power of manifestation. With a vivid imagination and a gift for seeing possibility where others see limitation, she helps business owners align their consciousness, expand their soul, and act with certainty to create extraordinary results. Donna Marie believes all success starts with transforming yourself first from within and then the world will match your transformation. With her knowledge of universal laws and spiritual wisdom, she's living proof that imagination, intention, and belief can take you on the most magical journey of your life.

Scan the QR code for More!

CHAPTER 11
UNLOCKING THE MAGIC OF IRISH TRADITIONAL MUSIC

None of us came out of the womb knowing anything!

- Tara Connaghan

• • •

I open my eyes, suddenly aware of the sweet chocolate notes of stout wafting from the nearby tables. I realise I've been in a trance, one that music frequently induces in me when I'm bouncing my music off the musicians around me. It brings me to an utterly higher level, a place that I cannot reach while doing any other task or activity. A place where I play my best music, and I am totally in flow. And it is addictive, my drug of choice.

This connection with something greater than me, greater than my music or any one person's music, is what drives and motivates me. I can sense and feel that it motivates others too. Not just the musicians in an Irish traditional music session, but those listening as well. That's when the room bounces, and everyone feels the sparks of magic in the air. It is an unreal feeling, like we are connecting somewhere in the ether, somewhere outside the realm and constraints of the room, somewhere outside reality.

Have you ever witnessed people connecting and building rapport? Or a couple in that first flush of romance - and you felt the energy ripple outwards? The honeymoon phase where the magic happens? With the right ingredients, a session transcends routine, and we can all be elevated to that honeymoon phase. Yet it doesn't stop when the session or music becomes overly familiar. We can continue to be elevated to an even deeper level where everything just seems to fall into place, and we play better than we've ever played before. I mean, how could that not be addictive?

This is the feeling so many musicians crave, and yet too few realise exists.

In pursuit of my curiosity to dissect the ingredients of a magical session and partially inspired by probing questions from my group of adult students, I have chatted with many musicians, from beginner to advanced and as much of the in-between as possible. Some of these conversations have found their way onto my podcast (and indeed are the reason I started the podcast) 'In Tune with Tradition - Perspectives on Session Etiquette in Irish Traditional Music.' I want to share those conversations so that every musician has the potential to experience true feelings of belonging and connectedness in sessions.

Irish music sessions are social gatherings and where there are social gatherings, etiquette follows. When we drive on the road, we find road etiquette, where we work, we find work those who breach etiquette. The word etiquette originates in France from the "ticket" or "label" which historically referred to rules for court behaviour. It is defined as "Customs or rules governing behaviour regarded as correct or acceptable in social or official life" and "Established customs or unwritten code of practice followed by members of certain professions or groups."

The unwritten nature of these behavioural codes is what people find most difficult to grasp, primarily musicians on their learning journey or musicians crossing over from other musical genres. Not knowing these customs or codes or even being totally unaware that existing customs are in place, can cause anxiety for those unknowingly in breach of customs and also for those striving to maintain an inclusive session. And it shouldn't be something that 'breachees' should feel embarrassed about. None of us came out of the womb knowing anything. We all had to spend time learning behaviours in different environments as and when we engaged in them. Irish music sessions are no different.

At a festival around the year 2000, I acutely remember feeling the struggle of not knowing what to say to a musician who joined a session I was playing in. I tried ignoring his insensitive behaviour until it reached unbearable levels. I then tried the compliment-sandwich method of addressing his behaviour, but I ended up receiving a fist threat to my face, so I retreated and suffered in silence for years. Many advanced and experienced musicians harbour this pain because they don't want to offend or discourage learner musicians or new faces.

The result? High quality private sessions behind closed doors away from learners or newcomers and also shielded from the spontaneous magic that can enhance sessions held in public spaces (frequently held in pubs) where you can physically see the excitement radiating on everyone around you. Ironically, it's newcomers and learners who could benefit most from experiencing this, if only the etiquette could be demystified.

I also remember feeling anxiety in my first year in university in the mid 1990s where I felt like an imposter, like I was participating in something way over my head and I received the feedback that maybe I should 'learn some more tunes' before I should join a session. Have you ever felt inadequate, like the weakest link? It hurts. And it can leave scars that our future selves try to protect us from.

But it also presents us with a decision. Am I going to do something about it – an 'action' that means I will address my shortcoming? Or will I keep experiencing this hurt and blame others – the 'inaction' of doing nothing? Or will I give up and move on to something else – a 'distraction' where I do something else to pretend the hurt is not there?

I chose action. I built up my repertoire over time and joined sessions without dread, but I went so far down the gathering repertoire path that I almost lost sight of my passion for experiencing the joy of the music, until a night in 2011 with the master Donegal fiddle player, Danny Meehan. Danny is a larger than life character with fingers the size of three of my fingers, having paved the streets of London for years, it's said he could carry two large paving slabs in each hand, but yet he plays the most sweet, delicate and agile music on the fiddle that you have ever heard. That night while sitting and playing beside Danny, he nudged me (almost off my seat!) to pass on the wisdom of his observation "Tara, don't you think it's time you started to enjoy the music that you play?"

His words unsettled me, and I had to hide that I had taken offence. The seeds of doubt lingered and grew more pervasive, eventually coming to the forefront of my mind at the next session. I wondered defensively and maybe a little resentfully "What did he mean??? Did he think I wasn't good enough? Of course, I enjoy the music I play!". But the pit of my stomach said otherwise. Deep down I realised that I was lying to myself.

I had been playing for other's approval, compensating for the hurt of not knowing enough tunes and of feeling inadequate. I had played what I thought I should, for those I thought were judging me. Not for myself. A bit like a musical "keeping up with the Jones's".

Have you ever found yourself overcompensating for past hurts or inadequacies? Or even for current hurts for that matter? We all do it, more frequently than we care to admit.

Maybe you attended a session in Ireland and felt like such an outsider that when you went home you stuck rigidly to the format of the Irish sessions you attended. "If I stick to the exact tunes and the exact chords, with the tunes in the exact order that I heard in Ireland, no one can say I am an imposter or that my session is not traditional enough. And I will make sure that everyone who attends the session will stick to these rules because this is what happened at a good session I attended in Ireland" with the result that creativity is stifled and smothered and visiting musicians feel anxious about joining or upsetting the current flow (or lack of flow). The fun and excitement are missing, and you don't feel the same magic you felt at that session in Ireland, even if you hide that fact from yourself and others.

Or perhaps you are worried about being the 'session wrecker', if you unknowingly have broken an unwritten rule at sessions on your learning journey. You ask about the rules but only receive vague answers leaving you more confused than you started and even more anxious. Your hands tremble as you fumble to start a tune. Is it the right time to start a tune? Are you allowed to start a tune? Should you wait to be asked? The anxiety is causing more anxious behaviour. Have you ever noticed that anxiety seems to feed itself? This can manifest in defensive behaviour, even if you know deep down that you are not a naturally defensive person. Sometimes sessions can feel more like a test than a celebration because you seem to be second guessing every movement.

Let's look at a scenario:

Imagine you arrive at an Irish traditional music session that you haven't been to before. Musically, you are fairly confident that you know a few tunes and can play along. Physically, the room is comfortable and safe. You look around and notice the musicians are chatting amongst themselves and it seems they know each other well. You don't know any of them. They don't immediately invite you in.

A small but significant sense of a lack of belonging makes you feel hesitant. You feel a slight tightness in your chest, the start of anxiety. You start questioning whether you belong "Maybe I'm not welcome, maybe I wouldn't fit in, maybe they don't want me to join but are too polite to say."

You decide to join despite your unease. You pick up your instrument and try to follow along. You catch a few notes, but the tempo and the rhythm seem different to what you're used to. You feel like you're losing your place in the tune and your anxiety intensifies. Then your fingers start to fumble and the tunes you knew well at home seem to evaporate into thin air and you're worried that others will notice your mistakes. Your palms start sweating and you can't even hold your instrument comfortably. You feel both invisible and painfully exposed all at the same time. You hear a lull in the session and think it's a good time to start a set of tunes. But you are so nervous you speed up until it's beyond your ability and you are not able to keep pace with yourself. What's worse? No one joins in so you are left vulnerable and exposed. Your discomfort feeds itself and you expect failure and rejection. You focus on your mistakes and they start compounding, one mistake and uncertainty on top of each other, confirming your fears and deepening your feeling of being an outsider. So, you start to withdraw physically and emotionally, retreating into yourself. Ultimately questioning whether you would ever start a tune again, and you may begin to question if you should come back or even continue playing this music.

Changemakers

I frequently see musicians struggle with this snowballing anxiety and that's why I created The Session Etiquette Explorer - a system to transform anxious beliefs into empowering habits, providing a framework where musicians can thrive, contribute and fully enjoy the magic of Irish music sessions.

So, let's see if we can change the scenario above with small interjections from ourselves and others:

Imagine you arrive at the same session. The musicians are chatting amongst themselves but one of them notices you have an instrument case. They nod and give you a warm smile [Interjection from session member]. You notice their body language is open [self-interjection]. Your heart rate slows, and you feel a subtle relief.

You walk over to the session and ask if the session is open to visitors [self-interjection], they reply that it is, and they seem to genuinely appreciate that you asked. This opens up space for more conversation and some banter between you and the musicians which you engage in and you tell them your name and mention where you are from, how long you have been learning and that you are open to learning more and receiving feedback if they think it's appropriate [self-interjection]. You start to feel like there is a connection and that there is good energy in the room. You join in with the music, your fingers naturally find the notes, even the unfamiliar tunes seem to start developing patterns in your head. The rhythm is becoming hypnotic, and you feel like you're playing better than ever. You are included in conversation with musicians between tunes while your music is being invited and respected as part of the group musical conversation. One of the musicians asks, "Have you got a tune?" [Interjection from session member] and you intuitively understand that you will be supported in playing that tune. You recognise it is not a test to 'lead' the session where you would feel under pressure, it is an offer of further camaraderie and support. You open yourself to connection and appreciation and this allows you to experience the musical highs of the session [self-interjection].

Everyone in the room seems to be feeding off the positive energy in the session. And even if you find yourself making a mistake, it is not a big deal, it is greeted with empathy not criticism. It feels like the musicians want to help you on your learning journey. Your chest swells with excitement and pride. Your self-esteem and confidence grow with every note. You feel like you really belong and you realise that it isn't just a session of music, you feel a deeper connection to the music and to the people, you have found your tribe. A tribe that nurtures, nourishes and challenges. You go home eager to practice and learn more, informed by the inclusive conversations you had with the musicians, and you are hungry for more.

As you can see, some small self-interjections and interjections from established members of a session, can transform a session and be the difference between a musician giving up or beaming from ear to ear. So how can you move from suffering the anxious state of the first scenario to enjoying the bliss of the second scenario?

I believe when you master the subtle art of decoding the unspoken rules of interaction, every session becomes an opportunity for magic. The Session Etiquette Explorer is an easy-to-use framework with 5 key areas to help people demystify sessions, using the acronym S.H.A.R.E. Sharing is caring. And Irish music is all about sharing the music and sharing the session space.

Decades of playing Irish music in sessions, stages, recordings, and teaching and mentoring have taught me this: the best sessions aren't built purely on flawless technique or encyclopaedic knowledge of the repertoire. They are crafted on understanding the social language, customs and values that have been passed on from generation to generation, that underpin all types of communities.

As experienced musicians, it is selfish to withhold wisdom. But learners must come with a willingness to grow so that the experienced musicians can facilitate and nurture their journey. When Irish traditional music practitioners help each other achieve greatness, we can all experience musical highs. The session can be a sacred space to SHARE our music, which is how this practice lives and grows.

If you sometimes feel anxious or you crave greater joy in an Irish music session, I invite you to listen to the podcast 'In Tune with Tradition, Perspectives on Session Etiquette in Irish Traditional Music', visit www.sessionetiquette.com or simply scan the QR code below to take a short self-assessment to discover your strengths, identify areas for growth and unlock resources to ignite your journey.

Tara Connaghan is a highly regarded fiddle player and podcaster from Glenties, Co. Donegal, in the Northwest of Ireland. She has been an active performer in the traditional music scene for over 30 years and is widely respected for both her artistry and her work in promoting Irish culture.

Tara is a founding member of the all-female, 13-strong Donegal fiddle collective SíFiddlers, which includes renowned musicians such as Mairéad Ní Mhaonaigh, Liz Doherty, Bríd Harper, Róisín Harrigan and Clare Friel and have attracted front-page national media coverage for their headlining concerts.

In 2025, Tara took on the bold task of examining the often-controversial topic of session etiquette. She launched the podcast In Tune with Tradition – Perspectives on Session Etiquette in Irish Traditional Music, which quickly established itself as an important platform for open conversation within the traditional music community.

Her contribution to Irish traditional music was recognised in 2024, when she was honoured as the Festival Guest of Honour at the Cup of Tae Festival in Ardara. That same weekend, Cairdeas na bhFidiléirí, of which Tara is a board member, received the Outstanding Contribution Award at the TG4 Gradam Ceoil Awards. She has also released the well-received album The Far Side of the Glen with fellow Donegal fiddler Derek McGinley, appeared on multiple recordings, and featured in over 40 television programmes, including presenting TG4's Geantraí. Tara studied music at University College Cork and completed the inaugural Masters in Irish Traditional Music Performance at the University of Limerick. She also holds a Postgraduate Diploma in Arts Administration and undertook a three-year programme with Na Píobairí Uilleann, learning the craft of uilleann pipe making.

Beyond performance, Tara has worked extensively in arts management and advocacy. She has served as Festival Director of Carlow Arts Festival, worked as a Traditional Arts Specialist with Clare County Council Arts Office, and as a Deis Advisor with the Arts Council of Ireland. With a broad curiosity across artforms, she is especially interested in the creative thought processes that connect music and other disciplines.

Following the death of her father in 2014, Tara took over her family's construction business, becoming the only woman in Ireland at the time to head such a company. Under her leadership, the firm specialised almost exclusively in large-scale civil projects for ESB Networks, building electrical substations nationwide. Despite these demanding responsibilities, she continued to perform and teach in a limited capacity. In June 2022, she began transitioning out of the construction industry to devote herself fully once more to her lifelong passion for music, cultural engagement, and creative legacy.

Scan here to begin your Session Assessment and unlock resources.

CHANGE
MAKERS
ENTREPRENEURS WITH A MISSION
VOICES WITH A MESSAGE
THE PROFESSIONAL SPEAKERS ACADEMY
UNLEASHING 17 VOICES, 17 JOURNEYS.
ONE RIPPLE EFFECT THAT WILL
TRANSFORM YOUR LIFE & BUSINESS.

CHAPTER 12
A JOURNEY TO FREEDOM

"Freedom begins the moment your company no longer needs you and thrives because your people can carry it forward together."

– Patrick Neudorfer

. . .

How do you design a business that grows stronger the less it depends on you? How might that set you free? How would it reshape your time and energy? And how would you use that new potential?

When I joined waldner partner in 2015 as a project manager, I didn't see it coming. I wasn't thinking about succession. I wasn't planning to take over a business. All I wanted was to deliver excellent work and grow as a professional. That was it. But once inside the organisation, I began to sense the weight our founder was carrying. The day-to-day decisions consumed him and the client relationships that lived in his head after working hours. I started to feel what it meant having a business depending on one person. Then came a moment that changed everything. Not only for me, but for the company as whole. I didn't inherit a business; I helped rebuild it from the inside out.

This is a story about stepping up, not stepping back. About a transformation, that took place through the courage of letting go, and ability to create space for others to rise up to the occasion. It's a guide to empowerment and for any business owner who suspects their greatest act of leadership might be to make themselves less dispensable.

Maybe you've built your own thriving business through years of hard work and commitment. However, if you're honest, your company might thrive only because you're an indispensable part of it. You are the one seeing the whole chessboard while others only see their own square. The tasks you delegate to your team boomerang half-done back to you, not because of a lack of talent, but because of a lack of perspective. That's why you might stay late at work to rework the other people's tasks. That's how you potentially miss a dinner you promised you wouldn't miss. You tell yourself it's just a season. And seasons have a way of turning into years.

Perhaps you are emotionally bound to what you've built. Undoubtably, you might have put your savings, and your reputation into it. So, when you whisper questions to yourself: "What's left if I step away? And what comes next?", consider it wisdom, not a weakness.

Changemakers

The question is whether you'll take deliberate action to find answers in due course to shape your freedom intentionally, rather than have circumstances dictate its terms to you.

Zurich. November 2015.

It's late afternoon in an office building in the centre of Zürich. The space is exactly what you'd expect from a firm that lives and breathes architecture: bright, minimal, transparent. The space is airy. Clean lines. Honest materials. It feels like clarity. But in a meeting room behind a closed door, something messy is unfolding. A man in his mid-to-late 50s with short grey hair exudes an aura of calm authority. He is a doer and a decision-maker. A builder in every sense and the mastermind behind the company he built. Dany Waldner is having a meeting with one of the employees considered for succession. A long-timer. A safe pair of hands. The conversation is meant to be the next step towards a carefully designed handover.

After an hour of tense deliberations, the colleague says at last, "Dany, I'm afraid I can't do this anymore. It's too much for me. The pressure, the expectations. I thought I could step into your shoes, but unfortunately, I can't. I'm stepping away. I'm out." The room falls quiet. The future that had seemed within reach suddenly feels fragile, almost imaginary. Dany's plan to gradually hand over his business, his baby evaporates in a single sentence and with it, the company's best-laid assumptions. His face changes. Shoulders that always carried certainty now carry disappointment. This is the moment Dany realises, there is no Plan B.

That evening, Dany goes home with questions no founder ever wants to face "What happens to my company if no one is willing to carry it forward? What happens to the people who depend on it?
What happens to everything I've built?

Zürich, September 2016.

Nine months later, the questions turn into a decision. It's a warm late summer day. Lake Zürich is a blue sheen beyond the windows. The air carries the scents of warm stone and early autumn.

Inside a conference room, 30 colleagues sit in a circle. Dany stands in the front, speaking with the calm of someone who has wrestled with hard truths and made his choice.

"I want the company to continue without me," he says. "Handing it over to the family is not an option. I also don't want to sell to outsiders. The people who shaped this place until this point, should also be able to shape its future. By 2020, you will have the chance to own this company." The words land heavily. Silence. Doubt. Curiosity. Some look startled; others sceptical. What once seemed like a straightforward succession is now an invitation to create something entirely new.

For Dany, this is the moment of letting go. Not of the company, not yet, but of the idea that one designated successor will carry it all. He is opening the door to another solution.

By that point, Dany Waldner AG was a well-known player in trade fair construction, general planning, and project management, with 35 employees across two locations in Zürich and Basel.

And me?
I'm sitting there as an employee, listening to Dany's words.
This is my turning point, the moment Dany's decision becomes
my responsibility.

Could we, as a team, really own and lead this company together? Could we prove that a business needn't depend on a single figure at the top? Could decision power be shared without impeding our progress?
At this moment something lights up inside me. I don't have the answers, but I know I want to try. In the days that follow, I talk to colleagues, I listen, I ask questions.

I dig into books and get absorbed by case studies on employee ownership, co-operatives, sociocracy, holacracy, and self-managing teams. On my quest for clarity, I hunt for tools and systems that help me understand how organisations are structured.

Changemakers

The more I learn, the clearer it becomes that traditional leadership systems are outdated. They serve founders, not futures. I begin to understand that we need something else. Something built on shared responsibility and empowerment, not on inherited positions. So, I start sketching organisational structures. Eventually, I step forward. That is the moment I choose to stop watching from the sidelines and start designing the future. Not just mine, ours. So with a team of first movers, we pitch this idea to Dany. Dany is convinced that ownership is not just about shares, it is about stewardship. He sees that real continuity comes not from appointing a single successor, but from distributing responsibility across many shoulders. Empowered by Dany's trust, we moved forward, shaping what would become a new organisational model.

Zürich, 2017-2020

In all honesty the next years weren't always easy.

People left. Some didn't want the responsibility that ownership implies. Others didn't trust the model without a boss at the top. At times, even I questioned whether we were on the right path. We made mistakes. We over-consulted on some decisions and under-communicated on others. But most importantly, we learned.

In the meantime, critics didn't hold back:
"Employee-owners? You'll regret it."
"Who makes the hard calls when it's ugly?"
"Fine in theory, impossible in practice."

And yet, quietly, something shifted. People began stepping up. They asked better questions. Not just about their tasks, but about intended outcomes, priorities, and delivered value. The company grew stronger because more people started pulling their weight.

And Dany? Still on board, not as the central node, but as a vital contributor, mentor, and peer in a shared system. That alone is a radical act of leadership. It takes courage to trade control for legacy.

On 1st July 2020, we officially became the co-operative waldner partner. Today, we run a healthy, and successful business.

But the real hallmark of achievement is our resilience. During the pandemic we encountered our greatest test to date. Many companies went into survival mode. We did something counter-intuitive, we launched a new business unit. That decision didn't come from a heroic founder's hunch. It came from a system where many people felt empowered to keep the finger on the pulse, propose new initiatives, and take responsibility. The lesson I learned is, in a crisis, distributed ownership breeds resilience.

That's why today we are successfully steering the company. Together. And the best part? Since the beginning of our journey, our transformation has been featured in various articles and podcasts and even documented in a case-study book. In 2022, our successful transformation was even recognised with the Swiss HR Award in Culture & Change.

That's the reason why today, my inbox bursts with e-mails containing the same question: How did you do this so successfully?

This transformation became a conviction and that conviction crystallised into a framework I now teach, the Successful Successor System. It helps owners design their own journey to freedom while elevating their people to carry the business beyond them. It's not a theory; it's a concrete blueprint of what worked, what didn't, and what I would do again.

Over the years, it has become unmistakably clear for me. The key to a successful business is building a company that doesn't depend on any single individual.

And the way to do that? Employee empowerment that is real, structured, and cultural.

The Successful Successor System™

The Successful Successor System is a four-part progression. I tell my clients that they can start at any of the four segments, however if you want momentum that lasts, I suggest moving along the system in order.

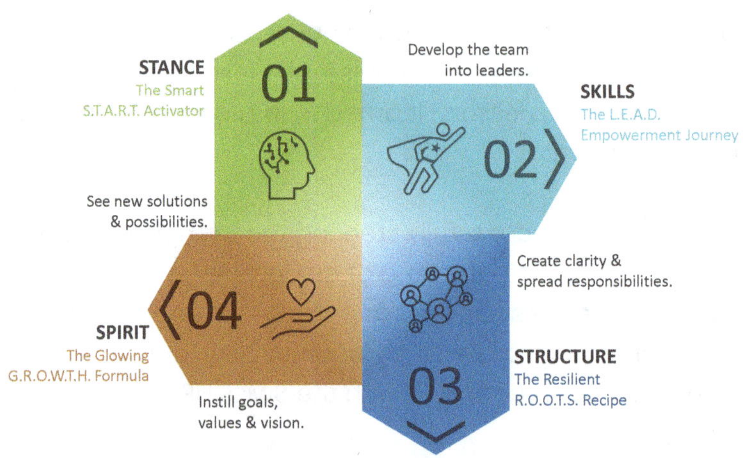

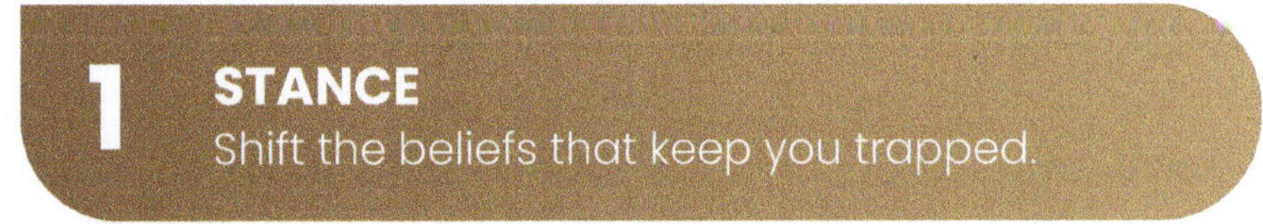

Why it matters. STANCE is your posture towards the business. It's the unspoken rules I hear when I work with business owners: "If I'm not involved, quality suffers." "Clients expect me." "They aren't ready." These beliefs make sense; they're also the ceiling of your freedom. Change the stance, and the ceiling will move.

Where owners get stuck. When succession starts to feel real, many oscillate between over-involvement and frustrated delegation. I notice that this is especially common at the start of succession planning. Business owners feel the need to act differently but don't know how. Without clarity, they're frozen in place.

What changes. I usually tell my clients: "Your business can only grow as much as you do." The Smart S.T.A.R.T Activator is the framework I use with my clients to work on those beliefs and break old patterns. It shifts perspective from doubt to possibility.

Outcome. As one client put it: "My role isn't to protect the business. It's to prepare it for life without me." After the Next-Generation Successor Summit that we organise, leaders shed doubts and start seeing opportunities and solutions they had never imagined.

<table><tr><td>2</td><td>SKILLS
Build capability at every level, not just the top.</td></tr></table>

Why it matters. SKILLS turn potential into performance. Owners often assume others "should know by now," forgetting it took them years to acquire their instincts. SKILLS is the bridge between your embodied know-how and your team's emerging capability.

Where owners get stuck. Unrealistic expectations. When a gap emerges, trust drains on both sides. Employees feel tested rather than developed. Owners feel reaffirmed in their suspicion: "I knew it. They're not ready." The cycle feeds itself.

What changes. To help build SKILLS at every level, I assist my clients with the roll out of the L.E.A.D. Empowerment Journey across the organisation. It is not just for managers; it is for everyone. It combines on-the-job challenges with mentoring, coaching, and peer learning. Crucially, it's tied to real decisions and value creation, not abstract workshops. People are taught to think like owners. How does this create value? What's the cost of delay? Who decides? What's the smallest safe step?

Outcome. Initiative-taking replaces approval-seeking. Meetings shorten and decisions crystallise because capability rises to meet responsibility. In our own transition, a project lead who never handled pricing strategy

took it on through mentoring. The first iteration wasn't perfect.
The second won margin we had been leaving on the table. The key
wasn't talent; it was space to practise and a structure to learn.

3 STRUCTURE
Remove bottlenecks;
make ownership operational.

Why it matters. STRUCTURE is how authority, information, and workflows
move. Without it, empowerment collapses under ambiguity. With it,
founder-centric heroics are replaced by distributed, aligned action.

Where owners get stuck. The bottleneck syndrome. Everything critical
routes through the owner "just to be safe". It feels prudent; it is actually
expensive. Opportunity slows. People hover. The owner burns out.

What changes. My clients implement the Resilient R.O.O.T.S Booster.
A practical redesign that spreads responsibility, clarifies roles, and
formalises decision rights. We identify single points of failure. We define
what gets decided where, by whom, and with what input. We introduce
lightweight, consent-based decisions to move fast without
risking the company.

Outcome. The first time a proposal passes by consent, "not perfect
but safe enough to try", you can feel the company breathe out.
Small, reversible decisions stop clogging your calendar.
Big, consequential ones get the airtime they deserve. That's how my
clients move from "Ask the owner" to "Follow the map". Clients stop
noticing who answered because the answer is consistent. You regain
headspace for strategy, product, or simply, life.

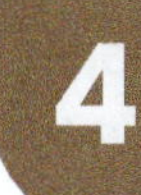

4 SPIRIT
Embed a culture where values aren't posters; they're behaviour.

Why it matters. SPIRIT is the lived culture: values, rituals, and norms that make behaviour predictable and relationships strong. In succession, culture is either your greatest asset or your hidden saboteur. I usually tell my clients, "The values that founded the business aren't necessarily the values that will make it future proof."

Where owners get stuck. Many succession plans ignore culture or treat it as aftercare. Misalignment then shows up as friction, politics, and passive resistance. Transitions fail not because the plan was wrong, but because the culture couldn't carry it.

What changes. My clients run Culture Design Labs using the Glowing G.R.O.W.T.H Formula. Teams co-create value codes (how we behave when it's hard), feedback formats (how we tell the truth with care), conflict resolution (how we handle conflicts with care and clarity), and celebration rituals (how we recognise progress). We make culture operational, embedded in hiring, promotion, decision-making, and client experience.

Outcome. My clients' organisations become flexible where they should be and distinctive where it matters. Values stop being posters and start being practices.

Together, these pillars turn businesses into self-sufficient ecosystems and owners into free agents of impact. We weren't just building a system; we were building successors.

The paradox of succession is that the more you try to hold on to control, the tighter the trap of rigidity. The more you share ownership with clarity, the freer you - and your company - become.

Changemakers

Looking back, the transformation of waldner partner, and of my clients, is not just about structures or legal forms. It is about people: how they grow, what they need, and what they give when they are trusted. Along the way, a handful of insights proved essential.

Insights that matter

Emotions
Change is emotional before it is structural. It takes time, energy, and patience, because people rarely shift at the pace of strategy.

Trust – Trust – Trust
At the heart of any change lies trust, built, maintained, renewed, again and again. Without it, nothing holds. With it, everything becomes possible.

Transparency
The more people are included, the stronger the system becomes. Transparency draws others in, creates alignment, and allows the company to carry more than one person ever could.

Courage
Waiting for perfection is paralysing. Progress requires courage: the courage to try, to learn, to adjust. "Good enough to try" is how transformation stays alive.

The "Why"
Purpose is the compass. When everyone is clear on why the business exists, decisions align and momentum follows. Without it, structures wobble and culture drifts.

Inner Work
The deepest shifts are inside us. Owners and employees alike must do the inner work: challenging beliefs, releasing control, and choosing a stance that serves the future, not just the past.

These insights are not theory; they are lived experience. They enable a business to move from dependence on one to the strength of many. They allow a founder to step back with confidence, and a successor to step forward with hope. Above all, they prove one truth: freedom begins the moment your company no longer needs you and thrives because your people can carry it forward together.

What we built and what you can build

A company without a single foreman sounded radical in 2016. Today, it's my everyday experience. We're a co-operative by design, not ideology, we chose the structure that best aligned with our intent-shared responsibility, shared reward, and shared future.

I started this journey as an employee who watched a succession plan dissolve in one sentence. Unexpectedly but with a clear intent I became a successor myself by choosing to design a company that didn't depend on me, nor on any one of us. The prize wasn't a title. It was freedom within a successful and thriving company, the freedom to be essential without being indispensable; the freedom to lead without being the bottleneck; the freedom to leave one day, knowing the business will go on.

If you're an owner, your greatest legacy may not be what you built while you were there. It may be what continues to live on and evolve when you're gone. Aim for that, and your freedom will come early.

You don't have to become a co-operative to achieve that. Ownership can remain with a family, a trust, or a partner group. What matters is that operational ownership, decision rights, accountability, capability and know-how are distributed, not concentrated with a handful of key people. The legal structure of the company can support the philosophy, but it does not replace it.

Changemakers

If you are an owner contemplating your next chapter, here are some uncomfortable truths intended as an invitation to reflect:

*   You cannot delegate responsibility while hoarding authority.
*   You cannot empower people with lofty speeches; you must redesign the system.
*   You cannot create successors if your business model requires a hero.

The path is learnable. It starts with STANCE, becomes visible through SKILLS, becomes sustainable through STRUCTURE, and becomes unstoppable through SPIRIT.

My invitation to you: Do not just plan your succession. Design it! Create a company that grows stronger the less it depends on you. Build an organisation that secures both your legacy and your freedom, while unlocking new value and growth for the people who carry it forward. If this speaks to you, let's talk. I'll share what I've learned and together we will explore what your path could look like.

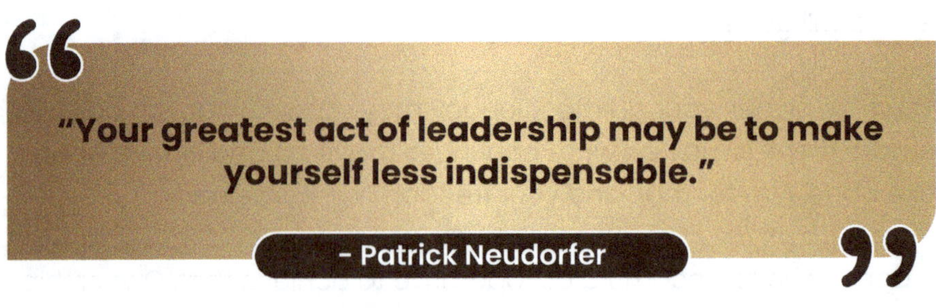

Patrick Neudorfer born 1983 is an architect, entrepreneur, business adviser, and change-maker. He has always been drawn to change, not out of desire to stem the tide, but driven to make sense of it, connect the dots, and guide through uncertainty with passion, clarity, and poise.

His career began as an architect, with professional experience in Austria, China, and now Switzerland. Over the years, Patrick has spearheaded numerous large and complex construction projects, skilfully aligning diverse interests and navigating complexity with steadiness. He quickly realised that every building project, at its core, is a change project. That's why he believes real progress doesn't stem from rigid plans, but flows from deep listening, alignment, and empathetic leadership. His strength lies in reading the room, understanding the needs, and helping teams move forward, together.

But his work didn't stop at commercial real estate. These same strengths became invaluable when he played the leading role in a business transformation. Starting as an employee and eventually becoming successor and co-owner of the employee-owned co-operative waldner partner in 2020.

This unique journey of transformation was recognised by the Swiss HR Award 2022 in the category Culture & Change. It revealed something greater than Patrick had imagined.

Inspired by this experience and leveraging his deeper understanding of leadership, ownership, and legacy, Patrick developed the Successful Successor System. A framework that helps business owners shape the future, empower their people, and build organisations that thrive beyond themselves. Today, he supports entrepreneurs navigating succession, and implementing structural, and cultural change.

He believes the best positioned companies for the future are the ones that empower driven individuals to take ownership, combining real leadership with resilient structures to create lasting impact, not just for today, but for the generations to come.

Scan the
QR code for
More!

CHANGE MAKERS
ENTREPRENEURS WITH A MISSION
VOICES WITH A MESSAGE
THE PROFESSIONAL SPEAKERS ACADEMY
UNLEASHING 17 VOICES, 17 JOURNEYS.
ONE RIPPLE EFFECT THAT WILL
TRANSFORM YOUR LIFE & BUSINESS.

CHAPTER 13
BUILT TO
RUN
WITHOUT YOU

Real freedom in business begins the moment you stop being its engine and start being its architect.

\- Andy Hooper

It's past midnight again.

The glow of my laptop screen is the only light in the room, my wife asleep upstairs. I'm on Google, typing the same phrases I've typed countless times before:

"How to be a CEO."

"How to get out of the daily grind."

"How to work on the business, not in it."

Click. Read. Disappointed. There's nothing real out there, nothing complete, practical, or proven. Just vague advice, motivational soundbites, and overpromises. No actual framework that could help me escape the trap I'd built for myself.

Because that's the truth, I built the trap.

Like so many owners, I believed I had to be involved in every decision, every day. I started my business for freedom yet chained myself to it. My phone never stopped. Every question, every approval, every fire to put out, it all came through me. I wasn't running a company; I was babysitting one.

And here's the kicker: it became my comfort zone. I knew how to work in the business. I'd never learned how to lead it without being inside it. Holidays weren't a relief, they were stressful missions. I'd sit on a beach with my phone in one hand, scanning emails for disaster, while Becki read a novel beside me. Even when I was "away," I was always there. Burnout doesn't always look like 90-hour weeks. Sometimes it's quieter, it's when you dread showing up. When you feel short-tempered, flat, and disconnected from the thing you built. You're not leading anymore; you're enduring.

One night, staring at the ceiling, it hit me, nobody's coming to fix this. If I wanted out, I'd have to create my own way out. That was the birth of **STEMS®,** a framework built in the trenches, not in a classroom. Five gears that, when working together, transform a business from owner-dependent to owner-free,

Scale. Structure. Systems. Stability. Synchronise.

Gear 1: Shift

Most owners think scaling means bigger teams, more sales, new markets. But scaling starts with you, the owner, not the company.

In April 2017, I was in the worst shape of my life, drinking too much, smoking too much, and carrying weight I didn't want. I didn't have the energy or focus to lead anything. So, I made a choice, up at 6:00 a.m., gym every morning for an hour. I listened to audiobooks and podcasts while training, what Tony Robbins calls NET time (No Extra Time).

That one decision changed everything. I gained discipline, energy, and mental clarity. And I made it a rule, if I wasn't healthy and sharp, the business couldn't be either.

The second part of Scale was alignment. In 2018, Becki and I sat at the kitchen table and mapped out a 10-year plan together. We agreed exactly where we wanted to be, financially, personally, as a family, by the time I turned 50. That alignment meant no more friction between home and business. If I needed to travel for work, she knew why. If she wanted more time for her horse, I encouraged it. We supported each other's goals while chasing shared ones.

From that point, my businesses exploded in growth, £100,000 to £500,000, then £1m, £2m, £4m, £8m+. And it all started with personal health, learning, and relationship alignment.

Gear 2: Structure

Structure is the foundation of a scalable business. Without it, you are the bottleneck. Every decision waits for you. Every small issue becomes your problem. That's why most businesses stall somewhere between £750k and £2m, they can't grow without exhausting the owner.

Structure means clarity: a vision, a mission, values, and a plan & budget that allow the team to act without you. When those four are in place, the business no longer depends on your constant presence.

When we invested in a warehousing business, the owner was burnt out, and the company was sliding backwards. We put in the Four Ps:

Product – make sure it was right for the audience.
Polaris – set a clear North Star (vision).
People – right people in the right seats.
Plan – a detailed roadmap to hit targets

Within 12 months, the business doubled, and the owner got his freedom back.

Gear 3: Systems

Systems turn your wins into repeatable processes. Without them, you're on the "good month, bad month" rollercoaster, some months booming, others scrambling to plug holes.

I break the systems into four stages:

1. **Awareness –** generating consistent leads.
2. **Close –** converting them into customers.
3. **Delivery –** fulfilling exactly what you promised.
4. **Consistency –** doing it at the same high standard every time.

We documented every process in the business, refined it, and trained the team until they could deliver without me. Systems stopped the leaks, stabilised revenue, and made growth sustainable.

Gear 4: Stability

Stability means profitability and cash flow strong enough to fund growth and reward you as the owner. Without it, you're always on the edge, scrambling for payroll, late on supplier payments, stuck in survival mode.

I use S.C.A.R:

Systems & Software – track and automate finances.
Cash Flow Forecast – predict inflows/outflows.
Actuals – know the real numbers.
Reporting – act fast when things slip.

In one acquisition, we paused unnecessary payments, renegotiated terms, reduced debtor days, and increased prices. Two months later, £300k extra profit was in the bank, and the valuation jumped nearly £1m in a year.

Gear 5: Soar

Synchronise is the bird's-eye view, seeing exactly what's happening across the business in real time.

Forget 3,000 metrics. You need six, tracked weekly:

1. Satisfaction/NPS.
2. Leads.
3. Conversion rate.
4. On-time/in-full delivery.
5. Churn.
6. Margin.

Colour code them: red, amber, green. If it's red, fix it now. If it's amber, monitor. If it's green, keep going.

Once all five gears turn together, the transformation is undeniable. When we bought Expandly in 2023, a software company doing £250k a year and losing £10k a month, we ran **STEMS®** through it. In 12 months, it hit £2.5m turnover with a 16% profit margin.

When we invested in a warehouse fulfilment company doing £600k, it jumped to £1.3m in nine months.

The formula works because it was built in the trenches, tested on my own companies before being applied to others.

Extraction changes everything.

From an investor's perspective, a business that runs without its owner is worth far more. If a company does £1m turnover and £200k profit with no owner involvement, the owner's salary is added back into profit. On a 4× multiple, that's a £1.2m valuation.

But if you're still inside it, a buyer has to replace you, lowering the multiple and slashing the value, sometimes by hundreds of thousands. Even if you never plan to sell, extraction gives you what you started for: freedom, choice, and the ability to build wealth without burning out.

STEMS® is that gearbox. If one gear jams, the engine struggles. But when all five turn smoothly, the business runs faster, cleaner, and gets you where you want to go without breaking you in the process.

I built **STEMS®** to save myself. Now, it's the framework I use to save others from the same trap.

You don't have to live in your business. You can lead it from above. You just need the right gears turning.

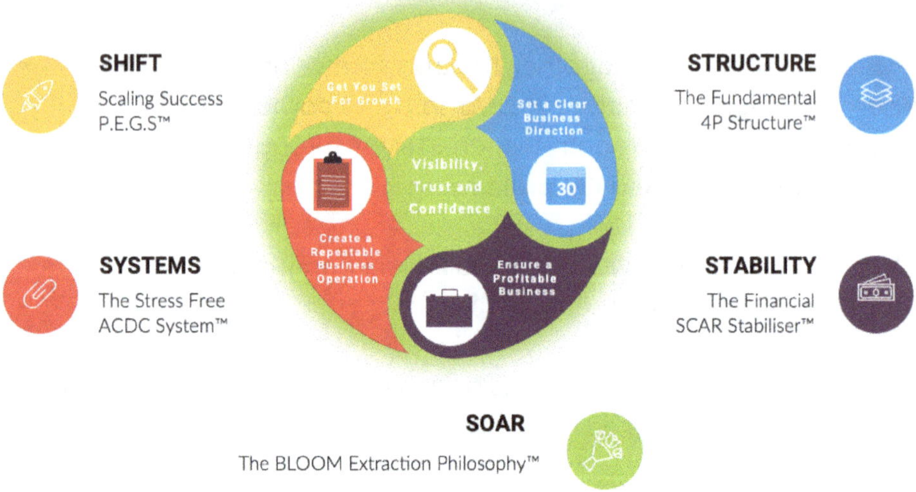

SHIFT
Scaling Success P.E.G.S™
STRUCTURE
The Fundamental 4P Structure™
SYSTEMS
The Stress Free ACDC System™
STABILITY
The Financial SCAR Stabiliser™
SOAR
The BLOOM Extraction Philosophy™
Get You Set For Growth
Set a Clear Business Direction
Visibility, Trust and Confidence
Create a Repeatable Business Operation
Ensure a Profitable Business
30

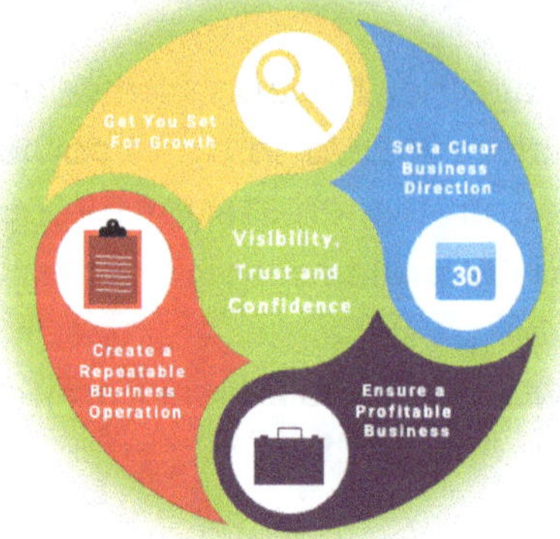

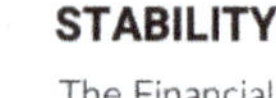

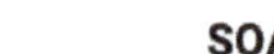

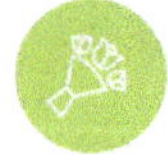

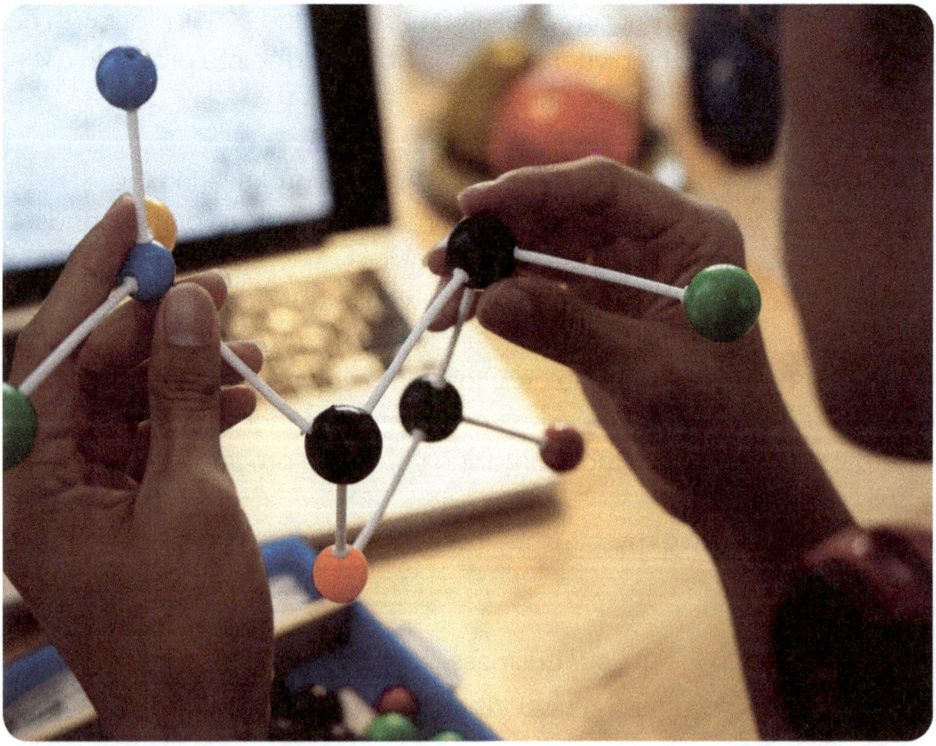

Andy Hooper – Investor, Entrepreneur & Global Expansion Strategist
Andy Hooper is an accomplished investor, entrepreneur, and international speaker, specialising in scaling e-commerce businesses and service providers into globally successful enterprises. With nearly two decades of experience in business development, consultancy, and coaching, he has built a reputation for turning ambitious ideas into scalable, sustainable, and internationally competitive companies.

As CEO of **Expandly,** Andy is on a mission to make international expansion simple and frictionless for e-commerce brands. Many entrepreneurs hit a ceiling when scaling globally, facing compliance hurdles, fragmented service providers, and limited infrastructure. Expandly removes these barriers by delivering the software, systems, and expertise needed to expand at the click of a button, guided by Andy's proprietary **Global Expansion Pathway®.**

Through GEE Capital, Andy also acquires and invests in e-commerce service providers and B2B businesses, building the ecosystem that supports global growth. By strategically combining technology, infrastructure, and specialist services, GEE Capital enables brands to scale confidently across borders.

Andy is the creator of the **STEMS®** framework, a proven methodology for building businesses that grow sustainably, attract investment, and allow founders to step back from daily operations without risk. Alongside **STEMS®**, his **OATS™** and **GEP™** models provide practical, results-driven tools for entrepreneurs looking to scale, systemise, and succeed internationally. These frameworks underpin both his acquisitions and Expandly's growth programmes.

For more than a decade, Andy has also inspired audiences as a motivational speaker. His talks blend personal development principles with real-world business experience, empowering individuals and teams to set bold goals and achieve their full potential. His approach is practical, outcome-focused, and rooted in the belief that the right mindset and strategy unlock limitless growth.

Passionate about supporting SMEs and emerging brands, Andy is dedicated to helping entrepreneurs break through barriers and access new opportunities. Whether guiding a founder through global market entry, designing operations for scalability, or preparing a business for acquisition, his focus is always on creating long-term success.

Outside of business, Andy is an avid adventurer on the water, sailing, windsurfing, or wing foiling, channelling the same energy and determination that fuel his professional journey.
Speaking Engagements:

Andy is a regular speaker at events including The Harbour Club, Hampshire Business Show, White Label Expo, and Payoneer Global (China), among others.

**Scan the
QR code for
More!**

CHAPTER 14

THE COST OF SOMEONE ELSE'S DREAM

"I dance where I was once caged – turning pain into fire, and fire into freedom"

- Krasimira Raykova

Childhood in Grey

What happens when someone tells you how to live?

And what does it cost you...when you listen?

I am eight years old, standing barefoot on the parquet floor in my bedroom in Pazardzhik, Bulgaria. The buildings around are concrete, square, one of many stamped across the town like copy-paste boxes from a ruler's plan. The stairwell smells of damp wool and boiled cabbage, voices always low, cautious, as though words themselves might be dangerous if spoken too loudly.

Outside, winter hangs heavy. Coal smoke snakes through the cracked window, clinging to the curtains. Everything is grey - the streets, the sky, the buildings, the silence.

But inside me? Inside me, there is colour.

I tie a sheet around my waist, spin in front of the cracked mirror, and imagine myself on stage under a blaze of light. In my mind, my skirt isn't white cotton but molten fire, reds, golds, oranges. My bare feet strike rhythms the walls of this country cannot contain.

From the kitchen, my mother's voice pierces the fantasy: "Krasimira! Don't be late for school!" I twirl once more, pretending not to hear. For a few stolen minutes, I can be free.

The music I imagine isn't mine; it's the music my father plays when the curtains are drawn tight. In secret, in shadows. My parents are the best dancing couple in town. When they move together, the air itself seems to pause and watch. My father's hand firm on my mother's back, her smile radiant as he spins her, her laughter light enough to melt the frost from the windows.

One evening, I sit cross-legged on the floor, watching them practice. I blurt out: "When I grow up, I want to dance just like you."

My father kneels, presses his forehead to mine, and whispers, "Better than us, princess. You'll be free."

But here, in communist Bulgaria, freedom is dangerous.

The Knock

The danger arrives one spring morning. The sound is not a knock but fists - relentless, pounding, rattling the door in its frame. My stomach plunges.

My mother freezes mid-step, then quickly masks her fear. She opens the door to two men in long dark coats. Their presence sucks the warmth from the hallway.

"You're coming with us," one says.

"For what?" my father asks. His voice is steady, but his jaw tightens.

The answer is delivered without emotion, as though read from stone, "Dancing to American music. Wearing Western clothes."

They lead him away.

I press my face against the cold glass of the window, watching the car disappear. My mother's trembling hand grips my shoulder as though to hold both of us upright.

Eight months later, he returns thinner, quieter, his eyes shadowed. The music in our house becomes no more than a whisper.
And the rules change.

"Don't dream too much, it only makes life harder" my mother warns while folding laundry.

"Be strong. Be useful" my father adds, staring into his tea.

And then, the sharpest cut of all, "Never trust a man. All men are the same."

I nod, obedient. But inside, the little girl who wanted to dance curls up and hides. From that day on, I become the girl who excels at school, who never causes trouble, who is useful. Even when I turned sixteen our married neighbour pretends to be one of my father's best friends and tried to rape me...I defended myself and kept it quiet....but I still remember that corner in my bedroom and his smelly breath of cigarettes and alcohol.

At nineteen, I marry at a ridiculously young age, not out of love, but out of duty. "That's what good girls do" my mother insists, and I so desperately wanted to be good.

I begin to pour myself into duty, into survival, into proving I'm enough.

Libya: A Cinematic Fear

This was a time when my hunger for survival almost cost me my freedom. At twenty-seven, working abroad to support my family, sending money home across borders, often through jobs that blurred the lines of legality. My son was only 6 months old when I began work illegally in Cyprus, behind a bar. Hearing the word "Police" I had two choices, to hide in the toilet or run out through the back door.

Then Tripoli, Libya. "Sukra Private Hospital" as a register nurse. My days are long, wrapped in long sleeves and skirts, adapting to a culture so far from my own. My passport locked with the Manager of the Hospital. Then one afternoon, a limousine with tinted windows pulls up outside. A man and woman step out and point directly at me.

"Come."

Changemakers

"Why?" I ask, my heart already hammering.

The woman replies softly: "We are taking you to a special hospital."
But when the gates open, I realise where I am, the palace. Tanks.
Rifles. Soldiers.

We are searched by towering female bodyguards, then ushered into a
cold, sterile room. Seven women. Waiting. Knowing.

And then, he enters. Muammar Gaddafi.

Tall. Slim. In a tracksuit. Eyes like black ice. He stops in front of me.
"What is your name?"

Then, without pause, "You will work for me and my family as a nurse."
I shiver, but my voice stays steady. "That is impossible.
My son is with me here."

He moves on, but later the conditions arrive like shackles, "If you work for
me, you cannot go to parties. You cannot speak of what you see. If I call
at one in the morning, you must be ready within thirty minutes.
Can you imagine? Me, wild, untamed, aching to dance, caged in a
palace of control.

That day, we were fed and sent back to the hospital as if nothing had
happened. But everything had.

Two months later, after my son's school year ended, we returned to
Bulgaria, and I quickly divorced my husband. He took half of my money,
the rest I gave to my parents. Because sometimes the most powerful
thing a woman can do is say no to control, and yes to freedom.
I packed a suitcase, a few clothes, some photographs, and guilt so
heavy my hands shake. With £80 in my pocket, I board a plane to the UK.

Survival in a New World

"Start over. Work hard. Don't look back," I whisper to myself as the plane descends.

The first year's blur into exhaustion. Double shifts in hospitals until my feet swell, my back aches, my bones hum with fatigue. My English is clumsy, so I scribble words on scraps of paper between patients.

I am nobody here. Invisible. But invisibility has its advantages, it teaches you to watch, to listen, to learn.

Slowly, brick by brick, I build. I study property contracts late into the night, risk what little I have, and reinvest.

Twenty-three years later, I own properties across the UK and Europe, all mortgage-free. I have money, status, independence.

And yet, inside, I am starving.

The Silent Weight of Motherhood

There is one truth I have carried like a stone in my chest; heavier than all the suitcases I dragged from country to country. My son from my first marriage, a gentle boy with eyes like mine and the only child I have.

When I left his father, I also left the only version of motherhood I knew. Not because I didn't love him, my God, I loved him, but because I had nothing left to give.

His father, wounded and bitter, sharpened his pain into lies: "Your mother abandoned you. She doesn't love you. You don't need her." My son never repeated these words to me, but I saw them written across his face. In the way he averted his eyes. In the distance that grew between us like a wall I couldn't climb.

At night, lying alone, the questions pressed down like stones. Am I a bad mother? Will he ever understand? Did I destroy the one thing that mattered most?

And yet, another voice whispered softly: You cannot mother from emptiness. You had to leave to save yourself. One day, he will see that.

Still, guilt became my constant companion. No matter how much success I built, it curled up beside me in the dark.

A Mirror That Looked Like a Stranger

By the time my second marriage ended, my heart was already weary. Malcolm and I hadn't fought in any dramatic way, we had simply drifted, the space between us widening until it felt unbridgeable.

One night, I poured a glass of wine and stared at my reflection in the darkened window. The woman staring back was strong. Independent. Successful. And yet her eyes were strangers to me.

"What if this isn't freedom?" I whispered to the glass. "What if I have built another cage, only prettier this time?"

I had money, properties, independence. But joy? Connection? Love? They were as absent as the music my father once played in secret.

The Call of the Dance

It happened on an ordinary night, scrolling without purpose, that I saw it, FEMININITY RETREAT – MALDIVES.

The words pulled at me like a tide. Before my mind could argue, my finger clicked Book Now.

When I stepped off the plane weeks later, the air wrapped around me like silk. The ocean shimmered in impossible shades of blue, the sun spilling gold over everything it touched.

For the first time in years, I felt the possibility of warmth not just on my skin, but inside me.

The women who greeted me didn't ask, "What do you do?" Instead, they asked, "How do you feel?" The question caught in my throat. I didn't know how to answer.

That night, we gathered barefoot under the stars. No mirrors. No phones. Just the pulse of waves and the heartbeat of a drum.

The facilitator's voice washed over us: "Let your hips tell the truth your voice has silenced. Let your body become your home again. It is safe now. You don't have to perform. You just have to feel."

At first, my movements were awkward, my steps small. But then, something loosened. My hips began to sway. My arms rose. My feet pressed into the earth with a rhythm my mind had long forgotten.

And then the tears came. Hot. Unstoppable.

I cried for the little girl in Bulgaria who was told not to dream.

I cried for the mother who left to survive.

I cried for the woman who mistook hardness for strength.

Through tantra rituals, kundalini awakenings, and sacred dance, I shed layer after layer of armour. Each movement was a reclamation. Each breath a return.

"You don't have to be hard to be strong," the facilitator whispered. "Your softness is your superpower."

For the first time in my life, I believed it. I wasn't just healing.
I was being reborn.

Love, Revisited

When I returned home, I felt different in my very bones. The guilt that had always sat on my chest had shifted, lighter now, like smoke instead of stone.

On impulse, I picked up the phone.

"Malcolm," I said, "would you like to meet?"

We sat across from one another at a small café. For a moment, neither of us spoke. Then our eyes met, and in that instant, I knew, the love had never truly left. It had simply been buried under the weight of all I hadn't yet healed.

"I don't need to fix you," I told him, voice trembling but steady. "I only need to feel myself. I'm not here to lead. I'm here to love. And I finally love myself enough to be loved."

We began again. Not from need, not from duty, but from alignment. Our love is deeper now. Not perfect, but real.

Claiming My Fire

Today, I am no longer the woman I once was. I am not the frightened child hiding her dreams, nor the woman numbing herself with endless work, nor the stranger staring back from a window's reflection.

I am a certiffied life coach. A kundalini activation facilitator. A guide for women who are ready to return to themselves.

I created my authentic program 'The Radiant Feminine Awakening system.'– a journey designed to awaken sensuality, softness, magnetism, and power. Through sacred dance, tantra rituals, and embodiment practices, I help women lay down their armour, break destructive patterns, and reignite the fire that was never lost, only buried. These six principles are not theory; they are the practices and truths that helped me reclaim my softness, my magnetism, and my joy.

BELIEFS – Rewiring the Feminine Mind

What I see again and again in high-performing women is a familiar pattern: achievement without fulfilment. They are constantly checking boxes and hitting goals, yet still feeling empty, disconnected, and secretly dissatisfied.

In "The Radiant Feminine Awakening" System, I guide them through a ritual tool I call the Purposeful Passion Activator. This practice helps them rewire old mental and emotional patterns, shifting from harsh self-criticism to magnetic confidence, from burnout to joyful discipline. Most importantly, it reconnects them to their inner feminine fire, the source of self-belief and radiance that achievement alone can never give.

BALANCE – Finding Harmony Through Breathwork & Kundalini Activation

The modern businesswoman lives in constant "go, go, go." Cortisol and adrenaline pump through her body for years at a time, creating chronic stress.

In a safe, sacred space, I guide women through The Inner C.A.L.M. Creator, a combination of breathwork and kundalini activation that helps release trauma from childhood and dissolve negative emotions that no longer serve. What emerges is balance, clarity of mind, steadiness of heart, and a nervous system finally allowed to rest.

BONDING – Nurturing the Feminine Spirit Through Creativity

Let's be honest, many responsible, high-achieving women have no hobbies outside of their phones and their work. Their lives are efficient, but their spirits are starved.

That's why I created The Magnetic M.U.S.E. Activator. In my retreats, women tap into their creativity in surprising, delightful ways. Whether through painting, writing, crafting, or simple play, they unlock the joy of creating without pressure. Feminine energy is creative energy, and when it flows, a woman becomes magnetic.

BEYOND – Rediscovering Sexuality

Intimacy is one of our deepest human desires, and yet it is also where many women carry the most shame.

Ambitious women often live in logic and responsibility, pushing sensuality aside. Their bodies tighten, their pleasure is suppressed, their libido fades. Through my sacred A.P.H.R.O.D.I.T.E. Attractor Method, I help women release shame around desire and sexuality. With rituals, exercises, and sacred feminine teachings, they awaken pleasure and reclaim confidence in their bodies. They learn that their sensuality is not a weakness, but a divine power.

BEAUTY – Radiance as Success

So many women know how to succeed by doing more, but the next level of success comes not from effort, it comes from radiance.

In The Cleopatra Secrets Code, I teach women to nourish their bodies, embrace ancient beauty rituals, and unlock their natural glow. When they lead from their radiance instead of just their résumé, they become unforgettable. Their presence influences more than their words ever could.

BELOVED – The Mystery of Relationships and Magnetic Communication

Masculine energy often serves women well in business, but in relationships, it can create imbalance. They either attract emotionally unavailable men or find themselves over-giving, over-controlling, and quietly resentful.

In my program, The P.E.R.F.E.C.T. Partnership Protector, women learn how to communicate from their feminine essence and how to choose partners who honour their hearts, not just their achievements. They discover that love flourishes not in competition, but in polarity, when they allow themselves to receive as much as they give.

This is the journey of **The Radiant Feminine Awakening System™,** I know what it feels like to lose yourself. And I know what it takes to find her again.

For me, the cost of living by other people's expectations was devastating. I lost my joy, my softness, my body's wisdom, and the intimacy I craved.

But I also know this, those chains that once silenced my dance became the very fire that set me free.

A Word to You

If you are reading this and you feel exhausted from proving your worth...
If you have been strong for so long that you no longer remember what softness feels like...
If you are starving for love, for freedom, for joy.
Hear me.
You are not broken.
You are simply being called home.

Home to your body.
Home to your rhythm.
Home to your truth.
Home to your feminine fire.

And when you are ready, I will be here.
With open arms.
And a drumbeat to guide your dance home.

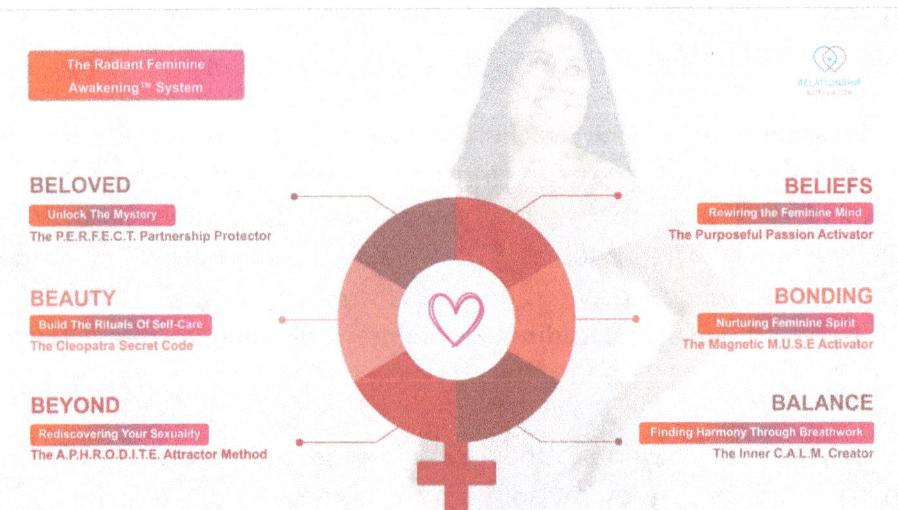

Krasimira Raykova is an author, speaker, coach, family therapist, registered nurse, and the CEO and founder of **The Radiant Feminine Awakening™ System.** Her mission is to guide ambitious women in releasing the armour of achievement and awaken their softness, radiance, and magnetic feminine power through retreats, workshops, and coaching. With extensive experience, including 70-hour weeks on the COVID frontline and managing successful property businesses in the UK and Bulgaria, she blends deep care with strength and vision. Her own awakening began at a retreat in the Maldives.

Krasimira enjoys traveling, dancing, sun-soaked days by the sea, and soulful connections in nature, and is also a loving wife and mother.

Scan the QR code for More!

CHANGE MAKERS
ENTREPRENEURS WITH A MISSION
VOICES WITH A MESSAGE
THE PROFESSIONAL SPEAKERS ACADEMY
UNLEASHING 17 VOICES, 17 JOURNEYS.
ONE RIPPLE EFFECT THAT WILL
TRANSFORM YOUR LIFE & BUSINESS.

CHAPTER 15

A JOURNEY INTO WHOLENESS

STEPPING FORWARD WITH GRIT, GRATITUDE, AND GRACE

"It all begins with a single choice:
to choose yourself and keep going,
one step at a time."

– Sheetal Radia

"You have Multiple Sclerosis."

Four words that change my life forever.

Have you ever felt like your world has been turned upside down? Just like that. No obvious warning. And you know that when the pieces are put back together life will never be same.

That was me. June 2004. Walking out of Clementine Churchill Hospital. Blindsided. Speechless. A blameless clear blue sky sailing above. The air hanging heavy with a myriad of unanswerable questions for what lay ahead.

I know exactly what MS is. It has taken a close friend into
a wheelchair overnight.
"What is it going to do to me? How is it going it affect my family? What about my children, what are their chances of getting it in the future? Will I be able to continue working? How long will I be able to walk?"

The gift of being diagnosed with an incurable neurological disease that is progressively disabling. One that affects the brain and myelin sheath, the covering which protects nerves along the spinal cord. No exact causes. No definite remedies. And no way of knowing exactly what will happen in between. A game of waiting and watching. Living with uncertainty is one of the hardest things to do. Living with threatening uncertainty is even harder.

Disease Modifying Drugs are offered with the caveat that at best they lengthen the time between relapses; aren't effective for everyone; the body acclimatises to them after which another is sought, and they all come with inherent side effects. For me, it seems like Russian roulette. Too many unknowns along a downhill slope.

For the next few months, I'm not ready to tell anyone; my friends, my family, my parents. I don't want to worry them; I don't want to be labelled, and I don't want to be treated differently. I want things to stay the same. Except on the inside, everything has changed.

My children are young. The one thing I do know is 'waiting and watching' isn't my game.

So, I hit the internet, and I am led to a book, MS a self-help guide by Judy Graham and in it I find Dr Kingsley. A GP well ahead of his time who has helped thousands of patients with MS, cancer and numerous chronic conditions recover with his holistic approach of treating the person not the illness. His advice being 'take away the bad things, add the good things and keep life in balance.' So that's what I do. Eat well, sleep well and travel to him for monthly intravenous infusions of vitamins and minerals. It works, the symptoms subside but here's the problem, a couple of years in he retires and I fall out of the routine of really taking care of myself. With a few dietary modifications I brazenly continue with my life. The times I overdo it I feel the repercussions. I rest and do nothing until they pass. My approach is working, or so I think.

I dive into my professional role as an architect and seize an exciting project. For six whole months I live, breathe and sleep it and to be honest it takes me away from keeping any balance in my life. I love what I am doing. My body does not. The signs are not outwardly apparent; they are simmering underneath.

It is August 2016. The project is complete with fantastic results, and I am flying high. I've booked a fancy lunch to celebrate with my family and as we walk towards the restaurant my left leg starts doing this strange puppet swing. With each step my foot starts to scuff the ground and just like that I nose-dive down to a super low. All over again.

This is downward progression. Not something I can ignore and if I do, I will be making my way into a wheelchair. My choices are clear, continue and let my mobility decline or I can do whatever it takes to keep on walking.

Denial, delay and distraction carry a heavy price tag when living with a chronic health issue.

It is 10pm in the evening. Everyone has gone to bed. The house is silent. I sit in my lounge in the dark. My heart heavy with fear. An endless stream of calculations whirring through my fragile mind. I know I have to dig deep. I have two beautiful teenagers. If not for me, I must do everything in my power to stay well for them. I want to dance at their celebrations.

I scroll endlessly on my phone searching for solutions and flickers of light start to appear.

Like striking a match in a dark place, hope springs up from books. In 'Recovering from MS' by George Jelinek and Karen Law. I find real life stories of hope and inspiration of others who, with the same condition at a similar stage, have ventured beyond the beliefs and boundaries of the Western medical model to recover some, if not all, of their health.

If they can do it, then so can I.

Time to go back to the drawing board; to live breathe and sleep the model of Holistic Health; this time to empower myself with courage and consistency.

Have you ever considered what empowerment really is? Is it something you are born with? Or is it something you develop over time?

Changemakers

And what is the model of Holistic Health?

Traditionally associated with Eastern philosophy, it works on the principle
of salutogenesis; building on our capacity to move beyond disease
focus and cultivate human flourishing. By exploring the underlying
causes not the symptoms; by treating the whole person instead
of individual parts. In contrast, the Western model of healthcare is
pathogenesis; the focus on managing disease symptoms, fixing parts
and pieces of the system relying on pharmaceutical
or surgical interventions.

Should you give your power away or hold it, nurture it and use it to
change your life?

I chose to do the latter and the more sustained work of peeling back my
layers began.

I surrounded myself with those on the same mission as me and became
a mentor on a Recover from MS Naturally group, a community of
people determined not to hand their health over to chance. We shared
knowledge and celebrated every little win along the way; a collection of
ordinary people quietly doing extraordinary things.

I trained to become a Scaravelli inspired yoga teacher. The focus being
on working with the body and not against it; working through it rather
than imposing preconceived ideal positions on to it. I am inspired to
teach yoga as a way into the body; to guide my students to become
aware of their ability to undo habits, remap movement patterns and
empower themselves with inner awareness to respond to rather than
react to life situations.

My real love is in exploring what lies beneath the surface to understand
the connections between mind, body and spirit. So, my training went
further and deeper to qualify as a professional yoga therapist. Yoga
therapy is an emerging modality in the field of lifestyle medicine. Its

focus is on a bio-psycho-social-spiritual model; on the basis that individuals are composed of different energetic layers – physical, mental, emotional, and spiritual, living together in community. It is a personalised therapeutic somatic process. A session is co-creative in nature, and its intention is to bring more coherence to the individual's energetic field by releasing restrictions held within and integrating any arising wisdom into their lives.

We are bound by layers of conditioning influenced by the culture we are born into, families who bring us up, our peers and the environment we inhabit. Our stories are woven into the fabric of our tissues. Our bodies are our biographies. The issues are held in this weave. Everything we put into our system affects us, whether it is food, drugs, relationships, thoughts, love or fear. Every choice we make has a consequence. There is no escaping that truth.

Disengaging from running on autopilot is a challenge for most people. It is easier to respond to the external stimuli picked up with our five senses. If we listen and pay close attention to the emotions, feelings and sensations that arise within us, we will find that our bodies are always talking to us. Issues arise when what may start as a whisper, ignored enough times turns into a roar, by which time the person is usually in a crisis and cannot ignore what their body has been trying to alert them to.

Our bodies are the containers. The breath is the medium between inner and outer worlds. As we enter the world, the first inhalation animates us. The last exhalation carries us away. And in between our lives consist of a series of breaths. A series of choices. A series of subsequent experiences. Every single day.

Alongside my thirst for knowledge, my daily efforts to recover continue. I have read countless books and have engaged in varied alternative therapies from homeopathy to hyperbaric oxygen; made changes in diet and have supplemented with high doses of Vitamin D; made lifestyle shifts from body brushing to brisk walks in the dawn light, chiropractic adjustments to cold water showers, resting and releasing toxic relationships, lots of meditation and movement daily whilst tracking my steps like a Fit Bit Ninja.

Every action and interaction has played its part in being where I am today. But here's the thing, nothing changes until you change. To truly recover and heal I have had to change from the inside out; rewire new circuits and shed layers of old patterning to shine my own light, whilst having complete faith in the innate intelligence that weaves in and around us. Every single breath of the way.

It has been an undulating path interspersed with extreme highs and lows. Light filled days when you witness an inch of progress; those extreme moments of joy when you feel like nothing is impossible. And dark days of despair that are an uphill journey. Times when the ascent feels so steep that all you want to do is stay stationary and do nothing. But when it's the hardest, it matters the most. That's the time to go in, to go slow and gather the reserves. To wake up the next day and start all over again in putting up a good effort to rebalance all that is out of kilter.

At times like this, surrounding myself with a kindred community has been an essential source of support. I have participated in numerous powerful workshops and retreats both in the UK and abroad. Time spent in these has been priceless. Whilst teachers have shared their evolved wisdom, the magic has come from the shared connection in community. When like-minded people retreat from their everyday routines and environment to come together with an intention of being rooted in deeper presence with each other, something truly mystical happens. People change people. We are doing it all the time.

There is a continual energetic crossing not only between the boundaries of our own internal layers but also those of others. Our energetic bodies are always talking to each other without even saying a word.

We are all the same, yet everyone is different with unique challenges and obstacles in their path. We are all journeying together, emitting individual ripples out into the world. Each affecting the other, yet evolving at our own pace. In this way we can influence but we cannot change the other. The work of inner change can only be undertaken by oneself.

In the final count, you are the only one living with yourself twenty-four hours a day, every single day. Nobody is coming to save you; nobody really has the power. Except yourself.

It all begins with a single choice: to choose yourself and keep going one step at a time.

Or in my case 3300 steps.

It is October 2023. 5am on my birthday.
We are some 3210 km above sea level.

2 days, 3300 stone steps and 25km later, I am standing ridiculously happy at the top of Poon Hill in Nepal. My children, adults now, are beaming at me with pride. My husband is radiating relief we all made it safely to the top. Trekking together along undulating peaks and valleys through sun, wind and rain hasn't been easy but every step taking us higher and higher has been completely worth it.

It is dark. The air is crisp. A crack appears in the clouds and golden light pours through to reveal the majestic Himalayan mountains. I am on top of the world, inside and out. In that humbling breathtaking moment, I am filled with nothing but love, joy and gratitude for being alive. I am also shown that ANYTHING is possible if you make a CHOICE to reach for it.

This is my journey of how little by little, through non-conventional routes, I am rebalancing my health and have achieved goals not thought possible. My walking challenges are not over, and neither is my persistence to overcome them. I am proud to share that I am not in a wheelchair. Instead, I have climbed mountains. Real and imagined.

Changemakers

Now I am passionate about helping people climb their own mountains. Whether literal or metaphorical, each one of us has a summit to reach.

We all have the potential to heal and outlive expectations if we are willing to become proactive experts and participants in our own health. To this end, it is with joy and purpose I share **The Intelligent Holistic Health Blueprint ™,** my compilation of six key areas to empower, change and evolve from the inside out. For professionals, business owners and executives, this programme, a combination of knowledge and practice, has been created for you to enhance your chronic health recovery and unravel the layers wrapped around yourselves to reveal your true brilliance.

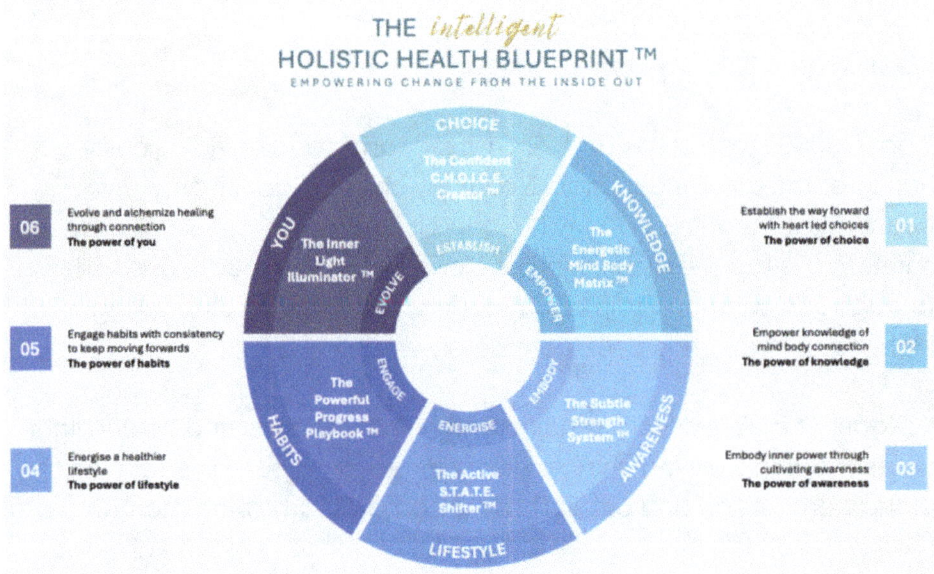

i. The power of choice
The fundamental starting point is understanding the power of choice. The Confident Choice Creator establishes the foundation and direction going forward with heart led choices.

ii. The power of knowledge

The Energetic Mind Body Matrix provides an understanding of the mind-body connections. Being empowered with this knowledge enables us to make full use of the resources within and increases motivation to apply action.

iii. The power of awareness

Awareness is the greatest catalyst for change. The Subtle Strength System provides key insights and practices to tune in to the body and make shifts within the internal landscape, to rebalance power and embody inner strength, rebalancing the nervous system.

iv, The power of lifestyle

The Active State Shifter gives an understanding of what is happening in the body in 5 key lifestyle areas. It provides information on changes which will energise lifestyle to take health forward in a positive direction.

v. The power of habits

The Powerful Progress Playbook provides tools to evaluate and engage consistently to keep moving forward. Consistency is the key to long lasting change. Once habits are rewired and the benefits become evident then motivation kicks in, sustaining momentum to propel us on our path of evolving and healing.

vi. The power of you

The focus of this final key area is on the social and spiritual aspects that make us whole. The Inner Light Illuminator provides key steps and practices for individuals to evolve and connect with themselves, with others and with the loving intelligence weaving in and around us. At the heart of it, it is this connection that is our true superpower and the alchemy to healing.

We are in constant relationship. With ourselves. With others. And with something beyond.

So why is now the right time to become a proactive expert in your own health?

Never has there been a time when information has been so rapidly available to us at the touch of a button. This knowledge is revealing to us that the world behind our eyes and under our skin is where our real power lies. So, it would be prudent to learn how the brain works, how the body functions, and how ultimately you can positively influence your own health journey.

Given what is happening in relation to the rise of chronic health conditions, the emerging model of holistic and lifestyle medicine has never been so important. Current data from the World Health Organisation indicates that chronic diseases are the major cause of death accounting for 75% of all deaths worldwide. That's a staggering 7 out of 10 people and the projections are rising. It is incredibly important to act now and do what you can to help yourself not get swept into this tide of statistics.

The old way of doing things is no longer working. There are growing communities worldwide who are engaging in holistic ways of rebalancing their health. Who are realising there is another way. It is no longer hippie or trendy. And alongside it, there is a growing body of scientific theory and evidence that is recognising that we are more than a system of parts. We are whole. It is a pivotal time in history where Western knowledge is merging with centuries of Eastern traditions and wisdom; where science is meeting spirituality. We are in the privileged position of being able to use the fusion of this knowledge, take action to put the wheels in motion and empower ourselves to become the pro-active expert engines in our lives to drive our own health forward.

Why is taking action now crucial? **If not now, when?**

Sheetal Radia is a yoga teacher (BWY), yoga therapist (B-CYT) and creator of **The Intelligent Holistic Health Blueprint.™**

As a Holistic Health and Transformation Coach, she empowers professionals, business owners and executives with chronic health issues to create change from the inside out. The knowledge and service she offers comes through her personal journey of transformation. After a diagnosis of Multiple Sclerosis in 2004, she has kept her health in balance holistically and has achieved goals not thought possible. Her story is a testament of hope, faith and resilience.

Sheetal is a proud mother of two and lives in the UK with a beautiful network of family and friends.

**Scan the
QR code for
More!**

CHANGE
MAKERS
ENTREPRENEURS WITH A MISSION
VOICES WITH A MESSAGE
THE PROFESSIONAL SPEAKERS ACADEMY
UNLEASHING 17 VOICES, 17 JOURNEYS.
ONE RIPPLE EFFECT THAT WILL
TRANSFORM YOUR LIFE & BUSINESS.

CHAPTER 16
THE ART OF SIMPLIFIED SCALING

HOW TO TURN A GOOD BUSINESS INTO A GREAT ONE: SCALABLE, VALUABLE, AND READY FOR THE FUTURE YOU WANT TO CREATE.

"On the brink of collapse, I discovered a system that saved my business- and my life. And has since helped thousands of entrepreneurs build stronger, lighter, more valuable companies."

- Sander Klos

. . .

The one and only question

The city fell silent around us. It was a late spring evening in Amsterdam, years before the word 'scaling' became fashionable, the air still carrying a trace of chill before summer arrived. I sat across from Brian Tracy on a low boat drifting through the canals. Evening light spilled molten over the surface, burnishing it gold. Glasses chimed; bicycles rattled on distant bridges. The tall houses leaned in, crooked and curious, as if the city itself strained to overhear.

I looked at him. A man whose books had sold millions, whose voice had filled conference halls across the globe. Now just the two of us, with one chance for a question. The question weighed like a coin in my palm. "Brian", I asked, careful not to waste the moment, "what is the number one source of happiness?"

His answer came with the calm of a man who had lived his words. He leaned back, eyes steady, and said softly, "That is an easy question. Of all the things people chase, only one prevails, peace of mind."

The words landed with surprising force. Perhaps because I was trained as a computer scientist, taught to reduce the world to logic, to debug reality as if life were a faulty code. Yet here was something no algorithm could fix. Peace of mind. I almost smiled at the disarming simplicity of it. Later, as I spoke with entrepreneurs across industries and continents, I began to see what he meant. Different challenges, different ambitions – yet beneath it all, the same restlessness. Not the lack of money. Not even the lack of growth. But the absence of peace of mind. The gnawing sense that the business owned them, not the other way around.
So let me turn to you directly. You have built something with your own hands. Hustled through long nights. Carried the weight of responsibility. You should be proud.

But does it give you peace of mind?

Because success is not working yourself raw while your family eats dinner without you. It is not being chained to a desk while life goes on elsewhere. Success is freedom. Impact. Legacy. A business that works harder than you do, so you can live on your own terms.

And if you are honest. Is that not what you truly want? A company that fuels you instead of draining you. A business that grows, scales, thrives, yet still leaves you time to breathe, to love, to live.

One path to that peace is Simplified Scaling, embodied in the 5FortyFive Growth System. Because happiness is not a destination. It is the silence between two sentences. The breath you take without needing to prove you matter. Because you already do.

And if peace of mind is the true measure of success, then it is worth asking, "where are you now?"

Carrying silent weight

Maybe you wake in a house you built yourself and instead of pride you feel the walls closing in. The rooms echo with unfinished tasks. The very thing meant to set you free now keeps you bound from dawn until long after midnight.

Cash flow pulls like a riptide, silent until it drags you under. Invoices stall, margins thin, and each new month feels like a gamble played with your sleep.

But worse than the numbers is the fog. Without a clear plan, every decision feels improvised. You move forward, but some part of you suspects the road is folding back on itself. You wake wondering if you are circling the same ground.

And then there is the sting of comparison. Competitors in the same market lift off like kites in a summer breeze, their growth seemingly effortless, while you drag a piano uphill in the rain. You wonder if they know a path you somehow missed.

Now picture something else. A business that runs like clockwork, breathing on its own. Calm at the centre because everything flows. A company no longer tethered to your pulse, moving to its own rhythm, delivering results you can trust.

See a client base that not only stays but thrives. Customers who praise your work, who speak of you with pride, who know you create real impact.

Watch profits steady and reserves grow. Cash no longer evaporating in thin margins but gathering into choices. Choices to invest in real estate, to protect your family, to scale on your terms.

And imagine the hidden dividend. The day you decide to sell. Not because you must, but because you can. Because you have built something that stands without you. A business lighter to lead and worth more precisely because it breathes on its own.

Beyond the numbers lies something deeper. Peace of mind. The certainty that your business lives even when you step away. That you can lead without being needed, rest without guilt, and live without chasing every detail.

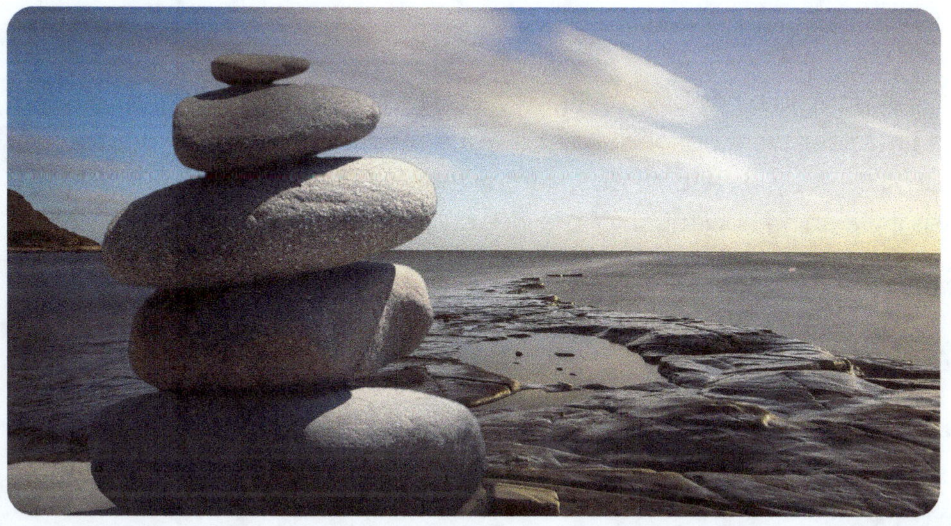

Changemakers

Do not build on effort. Build on a system. Lay structure beneath what is now instinct, your customer journey, your profit model, your team, your brand. That is where breathing space begins. To accelerate what works and to complete what is missing. That is what the 5FortyFive Growth System makes possible.

I know the weight because I have carried it myself. And one spring morning, it nearly ended me.

He studied me with professional detachment. "Stop, and maybe you live. Refuse, and you die." Then he turned and left, as if my life were a file to be closed.

The doctor's words pressed down without mercy, heavy and shapeless. For a moment the room seemed to tilt, as if the bed and I were sliding toward an edge. Not panic. Something quieter. Shame. A muted guilt, like being caught cheating on a test you wrote yourself. I had just made a big investment. Twelve people on payroll. A launch ahead. Everything lined up. And suddenly I realised, I was not the hero anymore.
I was the liability.

Walks by the Amstel. Books I picked up and put down. Podcasts I did not hear. The laptop stayed close, like a dog I did not trust off the leash. Silent. Watching. Like me.

One morning I met Oswald. Linen shirt, sunglasses, glass of wine as if time itself were optional. A serial exit entrepreneur, informal board advisor, early investor in IENS, and by then a good friend. He studied me as if weighing how much of me was still left.

"You need to do something", he said at last. Not advice. A mirror.
So, I called Jay Abraham, the marketing genius. Not for growth. For air. For survival. His voice over the phone was calm, almost casual, as if quoting a menu. "Twenty-five thousand dollars a month. Plus twenty-five percent of the profit increase." One sheet of paper. A lifeline disguised as a contract.

Together we stripped everything back. Not masterplans, just the basics. A clear client journey, plain and repeatable, something alive that could move even when I could not.

The team resisted. Too American. Too rigid. "Our business is different. Our clients are special." Yet slowly it worked. Clients renewed. Processes aligned. By month seven, sales equalled the first six months combined. Shareholders nodded. One of them said, "How many sales and marketing people fit in the office? Hire them. Scale. Push."

And then one morning I walked in and saw it. The business breathing on its own. A team humming. A rhythm set. No heroics. Just breath. Better than anything I had seen before.

What felt like collapse became the glimpse of something larger, the outline of a system that could carry more than just me.

From doubt to design

That morning by the Amstel was more than recovery. It was the glimpse of a system. A way for a company to breathe without draining its founder.

At first, the idea was dismissed. "Growth is chaos," some said. "You can't box it in." Others smiled politely and shifted the conversation back to hiring or product tweaks. A few laughed. "Systems are theory. Business is blood and sweat."

I knew those voices, they had once been mine. I too believed a growth system could never work. Convinced it would collapse in practice, I tested it on my own business, step by step, determined to expose the flaws. But it held. More than that, it worked better than anything I had seen before. Clients renewed. Processes aligned.
The business began to breathe.

Even academia resisted. A professor once withdrew an internship, insisting a universal, easy-to-apply growth system was theoretically impossible. The ridicule reminded me of Copernicus, scorned for saying

the earth moved around the sun. Theory said it was impossible.
Practice proved otherwise.

That scepticism taught me something, resistance is not proof you are
wrong. It is proof you are onto something that matters.

So, in 2016 I began testing the idea beyond my own walls.
One entrepreneur at a time. No grand promises, just the question,
would it work for them too? The first results were cautious but real.
A consultancy owner who swore municipalities never responded to
marketing suddenly saw steady leads. A small retailer who thought he
was "too small for structure" finally had his weekends back.

Demand grew. One company became several. Individual sessions
turned into groups. And in those groups, I discovered something
powerful, entrepreneurs learning as much from each other as from me.
What I thought would be a compromise became a multiplier.

That was the birth of Systemising University. Not lectures, not theory,
but four days of building, testing, refining, under pressure,
with skin in the game.

The work kept evolving. With our members we created the Scaleup
Tracker, a tool to project growth and valuation, making the invisible
visible. Writing TurboProfit forced me to sharpen it further. Three years
of work distilled into a field manual that gave entrepreneurs language
for what they already felt: growth could be lighter, clearer, predictable. It
became a bestseller and quickly sold out, leading to a second edition.

The simplified scaling system

What began as fragile outlines grew into five strategic movements,
refined until they could hold under any pressure. That system became
5FortyFive, a universal growth system for founder-led SMEs that turns
instinct into structure, so your company scales without you at the centre.
We don't call them commandments or principles, though they hold
things up as firmly as any Roman column. They are five strategic

movements every business must master to grow with ease and sustain that growth under pressure. Miss one, and growth falters. Use all five, and the system compounds.

Magnetic Market Alignment

Find the market already waiting for you. No shouting. Just resonance.

Unique Brand Magnifier

Your brand is not your logo. It is the gut feeling people carry when you leave the room. This movement clarifies, aligns, and amplifies it.

Magical Marketing Maximiser

Marketing is not begging or noise. Done right, it is flow, the right people arriving at the right moment, ready.

Profitable Business Blueprint

Your model is your silent partner. Shaped well, the frontend pays for the backend and profit replaces stress.

Client Closing Curve

Sales is not manipulation. It is choreography. A calm process that guides clients to choose with confidence.

Together these movements connect to the six growth drivers of every business. As I showed in TurboProfit, raise each by just 10%, more leads, more clients, more sales per client, higher price per sale, more products per sale, longer client lifespan, and your company grows fivefold in three years. One movement helps. Five change the game.

No magic. Just mathematics.

The result is a system that does not rely on your energy, but on structure. A business that works even when you do not.

Systemise. Scale. Succeed. That is the order, and the promise.

Wise-Up!

Inge Willems ran WiseUp from a garden house behind her home. Three team members. Local government clients. Around €600,000 in revenue. The work was solid, but growth felt heavy. Every new hire was a risk, margins stayed thin, and sales dragged.

She had tried programmes before. None had stuck. Her team had grown wary: too theoretical, too commercial, too far from their reality.

Inge herself had a master's degree in Marketing. She knew the theory, yet real growth remained elusive. When I told her about the outcomes of the system, she paused and said, "Then there is only one explanation. This system must truly work." That conviction pulled her across the line.
Her team doubted. "Municipalities don't respond to marketing."

"Our sector is different."

"Structure will kill our flexibility."Scaling systems, they agreed, belonged to another world.

But she started anyway. Quietly, step by step. Not with fireworks, but rhythm. Clear journey. Repeatable steps.

At first the doubts remained. But results came. Municipalities responded, not to campaigns, but to structure. Trust grew. Leads steadied. Projects flowed. Even the sceptical team began to lean in.

Next came the backend. Instead of one-off projects, WiseUp designed longer trajectories. Clients stayed for years instead of months. Margins grew. Value increased. What once felt "too commercial" now felt like clarity.

Today, WiseUp resides in a penthouse office. A team of over thirty senior managers and advisors. A client base covering much of the country. With their young professional concept, they built a key instrument for maximising front-end results. Multi-million buy-and-build strategies are now live options, with cash in the bank to fund the next move.

And yet in that penthouse, one meeting room still carries the name The Garden House. A reminder that pleasure and success are not distant dreams, but waiting for every entrepreneur.

When asked for the source of her success, Inge always replies, "I just follow the growth system as intended, without deviating from the roadmap. You don't start a debate with Google Maps when you want directions."

A step that could change everything

By this point you may be wondering how to bring the 5FortyFive Growth System into your own company. The truth is it is not a giant leap. For you, it is just one step. Small enough to take today, yet powerful enough to change the entire course of your company, your freedom, and your future.

And if you choose not to? Then nothing changes. The same late nights. The same uncertainty. The same questions without clear answers. You already know how that story feels, because you are living it now.

Changemakers

Not everything about growth can be learned from slides or theories. Some things you have to build, test, and feel in real time. That is why we created Systemising University. Not a seminar, but closer to a business hackathon where entrepreneurs step out of the noise and into focus. Four days fast paced. No endless PowerPoints, no passive note taking. Instead, live design, direct challenge, constant feedback that turns ideas into operating rhythm.

Muhammad Ali said, "Champions aren't made in the gym." He meant that real strength is forged in the ring. The same holds for entrepreneurs. Champions are not made in classrooms but by structuring and testing a business under real pressure. By the end, the noise has fallen away. What remains is clarity and a living blueprint you will actually use. Participants arrive for different reasons. Some are chasing profit, others calm. Some prepare their company for an exit, others for a legacy. Whatever the reason, the outcome is the same: a business that finally breathes on its own. If there is a challenge in this, it lies in the simplicity. Making something as complex as universal business growth feel as straightforward as assembling an IKEA cabinet is no small task. Hemingway once wrote that he did not have time to write a short letter. Years of testing and refinement went into making this feel light, while it holds firm when the pressure is on.

Simplified Scaling is not only about structure. It is also about leverage. Today that means using AI in ways most entrepreneurs never manage. Without a system, AI is just another experiment. With 5FortyFive, AI finds its place. Algorithms become assistants, data becomes decisions, and automation becomes freedom.

What we do not offer is fluff. No napkin strategies that vanish by Monday morning. We do growth that sticks. Systems that scale.
A business that breathes.

So, take the step. Join us, and the thousands of entrepreneurs who already have. Build the business you once dreamed of, lighter, stronger, finally free to breathe.

The future rarely knocks twice. Will you stand back politely, or walk through the open door into the future you desire?

The choice is yours. And from Amsterdam Airport, your next chapter is only a flight away.

Every entrepreneur dream of freedom:
A business that runs smoothly, scales with ease, and creates lasting value.

Not just more profit today, but the power to exit tomorrow on your own terms.

Sander Klos is an entrepreneur, strategist, and bestselling author. He has led companies through growth, scale, and sale. CEO of restaurant booking site IENS, later acquired by TripAdvisor. Part of the executive board that scaled fintech company Back base, now valued at over €2.5 billion. Founder of database specialist KRMG, sold to a London-listed firm.

As the founder of Business Accelerator and creator of the **5FortyFive Growth System,** he has worked with more than two thousand entrepreneurs to systemise their growth, their profits, and above all their peace of mind. His book TurboProfit became a bestseller and is now in its second edition.

He lives in Amsterdam, where the canals have often reminded him, that flow matters more than force. Those who work with him describe him as sharp, practical, and quietly reassuring. His own search for peace of mind has shaped the system he now teaches to others.

Scan the
QR code for
More!

CHAPTER 17

THE WHOLE SELF ADVANTAGE

FOR NEUROBRILLIANT SUCCESS

NEURODIVERGENT BRILLIANCE IN LIFE AND BUSINESS

You've never been 'too much' or 'not enough'! You are exactly who you're supposed to be! And you're exactly what the world needs.

\- Rebecca Mitchell Welsh

•••

Have you ever felt like you were built to think differently? And yet, you keep being handed instructions to life, that don't quite make sense?

And have you ever wondered how life and business might change if you finally had the secret manual in your hands – the one written for your exceptionally unique brain?

If so, you're not alone.

For so many ADHD, AuDHD, ASD, Dyslexic and Gifted entrepreneurs, professionals, and creative thinkers, the experience is the same, trying to succeed by following a manual that was never written with their unique brains in mind. It's following a neurotypical narrative, which doesn't include sidenotes or specific chapters for neurodivergent differences. It's no wonder everything can feel clunky, exhausting, or even impossible.

Maybe your brain feels like a browser with 274 tabs open - three of them playing audio, one about quantum physics, one with the latest health trend to come back to later... and another still holding a shopping cart from 2021. And the tab with your actual to-do list? Missing in action!

Or perhaps you sit down at your desk to work, ready to tackle something important... and somehow find yourself alphabetising your spice rack instead. That one urgent email still glares at you from the corner of your mind, but at least now you know exactly where the cumin lives.

Potentially it's not tasks but people. Getting out the magnifying glass and replaying every interaction like a detective. "Was I too blunt? Too much? Did I overshare again?" Picking up on feelings and vibes in a room is a skill like Detective Columbo, yet the overcompensating to lift everyone for peace is exhausting! Networking events feel like social escape rooms, and success looks reserved for super confident extroverts and polished social media influencers.

Changemakers

Possibly it's relationships. Misreading tone, forgetting birthdays, and needing 36 hours of solo recovery after one corporate meeting, kids' birthday party or a planned group dinner. It's either sending three paragraph texts at 3am or ghosting people for weeks. There is no middle ground. And then comes the guilt: I'm a bad friend.
A bad partner. A bad parent.

And let's not forget health. You know self-care matters - perhaps you've pinned 43 routines to follow, downloaded 5 meditation apps, and bought a yoga mat that now doubles as a laundry display stand. But when your nervous system is on high alert and your business and family life is pulling you in different directions, self-care becomes just another thing to fail at. Some weeks it's spirulina smoothies, journaling at dawn, and cold-water plunges. Other weeks? Toast for three meals and a cry in your dressing gown. There is no in-between.

What Does This Lead To?

- Unfinished projects.
- Missed opportunities.
- Businesses that lurch forward in chaotic bursts of brilliance... followed by mysterious silence.
- A constant background hum of guilt, shame, and imposter syndrome whispering, "Everyone else has their life together. Why can't you just do the thing?"

And that whisper? It grows louder.

But What If It Could Be Different?

Now imagine something else.

Picture your mind as a calm, creative studio - not a hurricane of papers, coffee cups and confetti. Ideas flow in, get captured, acted on, and completed. You know what matters today, not everything ever.

Decisions feel clearer. Your day has rhythm. Your brain isn't yelling "Do all the things!" anymore - it's saying, "We've got this."

Imagine starting tasks without the mythical beast of "Later" lurking over your shoulder. You break things down instinctively. They feel they will fit and support you! No more frantic all-nighters or inbox anxiety - just aligned action, at your pace, fuelled by clarity.

Picture yourself walking into a room - real or virtual - where you don't need to rehearse every word or decode every emoji. You feel seen, understood, not too much, not, not enough. You've found your people. You belong.

Envisage relationships that nourish you instead of draining you. Family dynamics that feel easier. Friendships where you don't need to shrink or over-give to be accepted. Conversations that don't end with you second-guessing yourself into the ground.

And finally, imagine health that isn't an afterthought. Rest isn't laziness, it's strategy. You wake with more energy, your nervous system isn't permanently in fight-or-flight, and you finally feel like you're not running on fumes. Your body is nourished and it's working for you!

So How Do You Get There?

I believe the answer lies in a Whole Self Strategy.

Because for neurodivergent people, success isn't just about mindset hacks, time-blocking, or working harder. It's about learning to work with your Brain, honour your Body, align your Business, and nurture your Bonds - instead of cutting parts of yourself off just to survive the day.

Changemakers

Taking a 'Whole Self' approach, enables all areas in life to complement each other in balance, and to thrive!

This is the work I do.

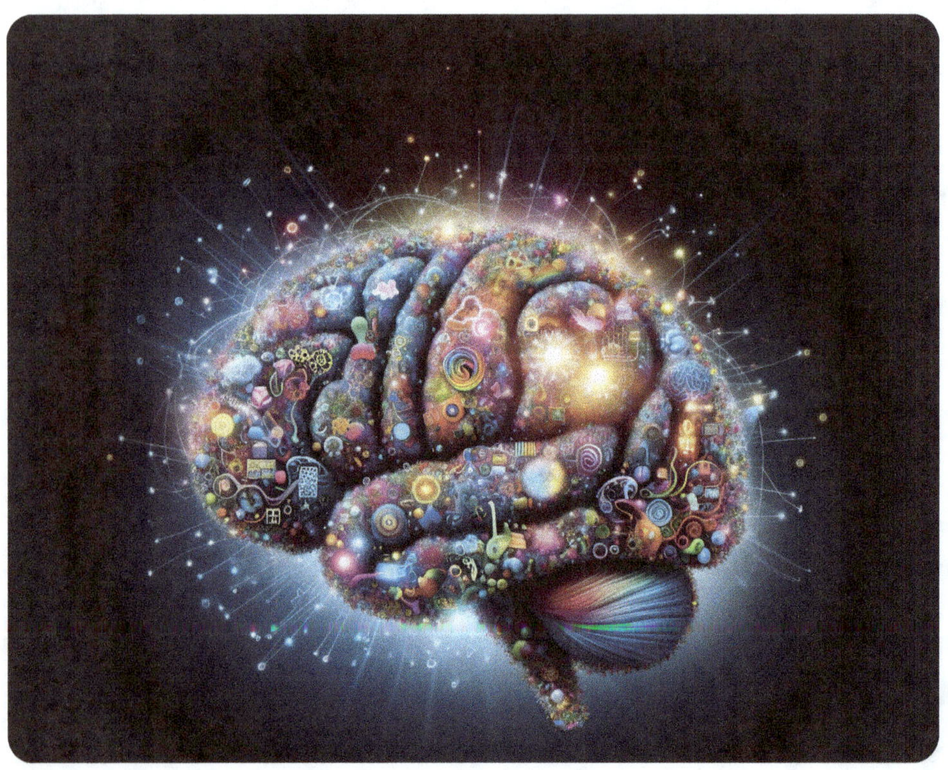

My own ADHD diagnosis arrived at age 42! And just like divorce... it's not an easy emotional road after the official stamp!

Navigating the "lost years", is a by-product of diagnosis - that's the grieving part - the realisation that I wasn't 'broken', and ruminating over the missed opportunities of years gone by and... 'what if' I had been diagnosed earlier...

I have vivid memories of little Rebecca ("Rebecca the Wrecker" no less, a whirlwind with an equally appropriate nickname as a toddler and young child), full of energy cartwheeling everywhere; growing up saying and doing the wrong things all the time it appeared, missing social cues with friends, learning to copy their behaviours and the start of people - pleasing; plus hyper focusing on collecting things, creative art projects and 'super stuff' - Dinosaurs, story writing and my football obsession are stand outs!

Teenage Rebecca was renowned for being late for school, forgetting homework and studying for exams at the last moment. Teachers said they were surprised I got the grades I did, and I felt shame for doing well. In the background, my sports obsession continued on the court and off, writing short stories evolved, and my own home projects became more important than homework of course!

University Rebecca managed to get a Journalism Degree, with hyper focus on certain modules and projects, but an avoidance for others. Everything was to deadline (in the days of lining up in the hallway at the Submissions Office at 3pm on a Friday...). And yet I had a high-achieving side quest as the enthusiastic, networking Sports Editor! Had all the time in the world for that...

Navigating my working life, I can see where there were struggles with day-to-day tasks and time management, yet as a creative and innovative person, this was superseded by areas where I exceeded targets, increased productivity and revenue, and was highly successful. Additionally, on the side quest subject, set up an online retail business, volunteered on the Local Authority Sports Council and joined a national 'Think Tank', to make positive political change...

Looking back I can see how I was always a very creative person, and I had a firm focus to make a difference! Did you know that neurodiverse people have a strong sense of justice? I was always doing something to support positive change, and yet I always felt it wasn't good enough. I wasn't good enough.

And then my relationships! My four incredible children! And then recovering from a narcissistic abusive marriage...

Changemakers

How did I end up here? I did a lot of work around this! I furiously researched, investigated and wrote, becoming a Narcissist Abuse Specialist and trained as a Trauma Coach. This led to becoming a number 1 Best Selling Author and developing "the Wellness Steps", a programme to support women recovering from trauma.

Following my ADHD diagnosis, I continued to research and write about neurodivergent people finding themselves in narcissistic and abusive relationships.

I became a Number 1 Bestseller again, in fiction this time!
I never gave up on my love of writing stories!

My side projects made sense, as I started to make positive change, volunteering locally, getting more girls into football, and growing our local Girls Football Club to over 100 members. As a coach, I gained my UEFA C License, Talent ID License and SFA Coach Educator Award, as well as joining the Professional Speakers Academy and training as an ACE Mentor. I found my voice! And I continued to serve and support others to make positive change!

And bit by bit, I started seeing the transformation of implementing changes into my life and my routine, with techniques gathered from all over, and this flourished.

This is the system I've built from combining research with lived experience. Bringing best practice together from training and coaching for over twenty years, and seeing how volunteering is a force for neurodiverse people! It is called:

The NeuroBrilliant Blueprint ™

This is a Whole Self Strategy, working with neurodivergent strengths, to overcome challenges, which enables living a quality and successful life, balancing all areas! The NeuroBrilliant Blueprint focuses on five distinct and essential areas that come together to provide the Whole Self Advantage!

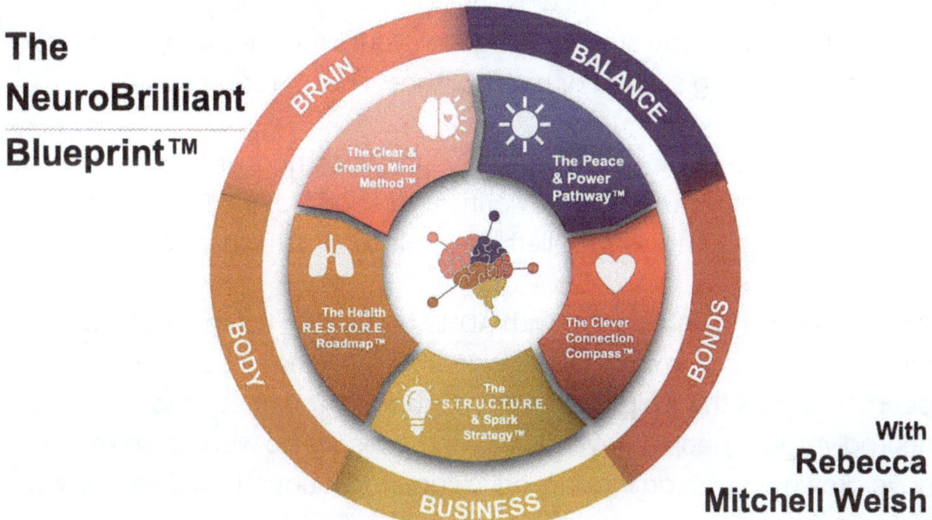

1. BRAIN: The Clear & Creative Mind Method™
Understanding a mind alive with ideas, creativity and unique strengths

The incredible ADHD, AuDHD, ASD, Dyslexic and Gifted Brain is different indeed, and has many qualities, and therefore it is essential to understand how to manifest this difference for a better quality of life!

A problem I see is that some neurodiverse people enthusiastically want to make changes in their lives and have the best intentions - plus a nice, new, shiny notebook to get started - and yet there's no understanding of how their brain works. And this means when it comes to sticking to routines, and the new way of doing things, it all breaks down because there is no understanding, the 'Why?' and 'How?'. This can lead to the negative self-talk and the downward shame spiral!

I look at it like this, it's like a separate operating system, kind of like how Android is to Apple, and you've been given the instruction manual to the wrong one!

I believe it is essential to understand the differences and how neuroBrilliant brains work the way they do. Can you imagine the advantages when you start working with your creative brain, rather than using an operating system or manual that is not fit for purpose?

That is one area of the Clear & Creative Mind Method, and within the Five Steps here - Perceive, Process, Prioritise, Personalise and Pause - there is focus on self-talk, mindset, beliefs and values, and reframing.

Did you know that individuals with ADHD receive an estimated 20,000 more negative comments by the age of 10 than their neurotypical peers? Imagine the weight of that. It's probably fair to say that all neurodivergent people have experienced this. It's no wonder so many have grown up with an internal critic shouting louder than their natural creative voice.

The problem with this is that significant negative comments while growing up amounts to low self-esteem, shame, anxiety and a feeling of being 'different' or 'not fitting in' in adulthood.

There is also a heightened sensitivity to criticism and is known as 'Rejection Sensitive Dysphoria' (RSD), where individuals feel pain and overwhelming negative emotions in response to perceived rejection.

But here's the truth! Your brain isn't broken. It's brilliantly wired and has been using a neurotypical manual instead of enabling it to shine in its bright way! What needs shifting isn't your worth, you've always been enough just as you are, it's re-framing your thinking!

Cognitive reframing has been shown to reduce rumination and strengthen problem-solving (Beck, 2011), and it is a distinctive part of my Clear & Creative Mind Method. ™

Personally, I carried that inner critic with me for years. Every time I achieved something, it whispered, "Not enough. Not good enough." The shift came when I learned to pause and reframe. Instead of asking, "Why can't I do this?" I started asking, "What do I need in order to do this my way?" That single shift transformed my outlook, and my output.

Changing the frame changes the story. And when you change the story, you change the outcome.

2. BODY: The Health R.E.S.T.O.R.E. Roadmap™
Awakening energy and restoring health through nourishment, movement and nervous system care

Through media and advertising, we're told to push harder, fuel ourselves on easy processed foods and caffeine, spend money on the latest health gadgets and fads, and then pat ourselves on the back that we're now officially healthy!

But the reality is, it's a sticky plaster. Ignoring your body isn't resilience. It's sabotage. It's like expecting your phone to run all day on 1% battery, eventually, the screen goes black.

Burnout creeps in quietly. It can start with heavy eyelids and growing brain fog. Then it's the irritability, the sugar cravings, the late-night scrolling because your nervous system won't switch off. And yet it seems the world claps you on the back for "pushing through", right up until your system gives way. Have you heard of Autism or ADHD Burnout – and try AuDHD Burnout on for size too?

I see energy as the foundation of sustainable success. I see that neuroBrilliant people have an abundance of energy for a reason. Without it, creativity and clarity don't stand a chance!

Changemakers

One study found that even a single night of poor sleep can reduce working memory performance by up to 40% (Lim & Dinges, 2010). And notoriously, neurodiverse brains are not the best at getting a good night's sleep as it is - the internal playlist starts and the inner voice asking whether the door is locked, replaying a conversation from ten years ago and wondering what penguins would look like if they wore hats...

Understanding these unique challenges, I created the Health RESTORE Roadmap to ensure the body is energised, to support everyday life and to resist burnout.

You see, I believe that neuroBrillant people were born with incredible energy, more than average people, and thrive through movement! We're active in our minds, with creative thoughts running continuously like a waterfall, and then there's the movement in our body with fidgeting and stimming, let alone sports and exercise! Ensuring motion is part of the ADHD, AuDHD, ASD, Dyslexic and Giftedness routine is key to vitality!

Nothing changes without movement, after all!

The Health RESTORE Roadmap moves forward with Nutrition, Hydration Gut Health and the Gut-Brain Connection, Hormone Changes awareness, the Nervous System and Vagus Nerve understanding and exercises, as well as Movement and Meditation.

Why is this important? Well, there's so much to consider in the body! And therefore getting a firm grasp of neurodiverse differences and effects enables positive change and rapid results in productivity!

This is what happened to Rachel, an entrepreneur with ADHD and Dyslexia. When I met Rachel, she had been cycling through late-night laptop marathons and burnout crashes. She joked living on "coffee, crisps, and chaos." But armed with new knowledge from the Health RESTORE Roadmap, she was able to implement effective routines because this made sense to her specific challenges, and leaned into her strengths.

A reluctant cook yet Rachel found a hyper focus! Exploring the recommended herbs and spices, and understanding their benefits, was a key element of finding tastes she liked, replacing artificial flavourings, and as a result boosted her health and productivity. And rapidly, she was calmer and more focused, and laughs that her the biggest win wasn't her productivity, it was that people stopped saying, "You look tired."

Because here's the thing, heading for burnout isn't a badge of honour. It's a warning. And when understanding neurodiverse differences underpins action, and you restore your body, you don't just get through the day. You get to live it.

3. BUSINESS: The S.T.R.U.C.T.U.R.E. & Spark Strategy™
Aligning personal strengths to build sustainable systems and success

It is in plain sight, rigid planners and colour-coded spreadsheets are often sold as "the fix" with countless Apps, Processes and Platforms out there promising the magical solution! But for many of us, they collapse within a week. It's like trying to wear a smaller-sized shoe, ok to wear for a short while as a quick fix, to hobble along, but very sore indeed and not suitable for the long run.

However, systems should serve you, not shackle you. Flexible, visual systems harness creativity instead of crushing it. Research shows that externalising tasks visually improves engagement and completion for ADHD brains (Clear, 2018). Therefore, one of the key areas in The STRUCTURE and Spark Strategy, is setting up business and professional solutions that fit the neuroBrilliant brain - and work.

Changemakers

As a Business Strategist, I analysed how to support neurodiverse brains in business and I pulled the key areas for success into nine skills to master: Simplify, Time, Rebuild, Understand, Clarify, Tidy, Use Techniques, Reflect, Execute.

These became the important ingredients for succeeding!

You see, neurodiverse people can struggle with organisation and expectations, drowning in sticky notes and piled up papers on desks, trying to stay updated using several organisation Apps, and spreadsheets open over copious desktop tabs.

Yet some of the most incredible change makers are neurodiverse! Albert Einstein, Temple Grandin, Richard Branson and Greta Thurberg are all recognised for the poweful impact they've made in their fields. They established structures to work with their unique brains, enabling their passions, creations and ideas to come to life and make positive change!

Focusing on the skill from Use Techniques, in the STRUCTURE & Spark Strategy, it's about simplifying and finding that one way to stay on top and in control, that works for your brain.

Far too often I've seen organising strategies start and fizzle out because they are not working for the neuroBrilliant mind. Through a range of Techniques, it's about finding the right one that fits you.

It's essentially a tailored approach in Business, and not a one size fits all policy. From working personally with neuroBrilliant minds, structures that work for one, won't work with another client – and vice versa! Just like all neurodiverse change makers! Therefore it's about finding your own strengths, your own personality, your own systems that will work for you.

That's the power of structure. Not rigidity. Not restriction. But systems that flex with you and your neuroBrilliant mind, and spark your creativity and progress.

4. BONDS: The Clever Connection Compass™
Creating Connections shaped by compassion, integrity and belonging

'Masking' can feel like the safest way to belong, hiding quirks or struggles so people won't judge. For neurodivergent individuals, this started a long time ago, to fit in, and be liked. And sometimes it is hard to see where the mask stops, and the true self starts…

But masking is like wearing a big fancy-dress costume all day. You might get through the party, but it gets heavy and exhausting!

Research shows masking is strongly linked to anxiety, depression, and burnout (Hull, Petrides, & Mandy, 2017). Throw in RSD and it can be overwhelming in social situations, friendship groups, work settings, business meetings, family gatherings…

Ultimately though, belonging doesn't come from performance. It comes from honesty and care. It is essential to be surrounded by people who understand you, for being you, as you are incredible as you are, with no mask!

That's why the Clever Connection Compass became so important! And using a five-step process: Connect, Clear, Create, Community and Centre, enables connection with self, others, nature and source.

Connection is essential to human existence - even though neuroBrilliant people can find this really tough to navigate! Although it can feel like two opposing magnets trying to fit together, connection is important in our family lives and professional lives!

But did you know that one of the strongest connections are the bonds we form with the natural world? Research shows that when we give our brains and bodies space to breathe among trees, water, sky or even a patch of green, something shifts - our attention sharpens, the invisible pressure under our skin eases, and life feels more meaningful (Jimenez et al., 2021).

Changemakers

Furthermore, a 2024 study found that neurodiverse participants experienced improved sensory-motor regulation, emotional resilience and a greater sense of inclusion when immersed in nature-responsive environments (Finnigan et al., 2024).

So stepping outside the meeting room, or pausing mid-scroll to feel the wind, or sitting quietly beneath a tree, you're not just taking a break, you're reinforcing a bond. You're giving your system the nourishment it needs to think, create and connect in a whole new way.

The Clever Connection Compass is designed specifically for neurodiverse individuals to feel connection. To build bonds that last. That are deserved of you! And supported by the right human connection! Finding your tribe is life-changing!

5. BALANCE: The Peace & Power Pathway™
Living with peace, purpose and power every day

Some people believe balance means splitting equal time between every role: business owner, parent, partner, friend. But that's like trying to keep a dozen plates spinning at once. Exhausting. Destined to shatter.

The truth? Balance isn't equal time. Balance is integration. Research has shown that integration across life areas or domains offers a richer and more health-promoting perspective and helps future outcomes, rather than rigid management approaches (Kerksieck et al, 2024). This is very helpful for anyone who experiences the symptoms of 'time blindness'.

So, balance isn't plate-spinning at all. It's conducting an orchestra. Not every instrument requires equal volume all the time, you bring different sections forward depending on the music.

In the Peace & Power Pathway, there are five areas to support living in Balance. These are Awareness, Anchor, Align, Adjust and Advance.

All parts here are important, and focusing specifically on the first skill, Awareness, is about recognising "triggers". These are indicators specific to an individual, showing a slight decline, or the start of losing balance, and can be noted across business or personal life. Examples here are: noticing that you are ordering take away food more often, or pouring another glass of wine each night (or perhaps finishing the bottle...) or maybe starting to skip showers, or increasingly staying at home to be alone, or putting off replying to business emails regularly, or delaying the kids' bedtime story ritual more...and more...

When these triggers are caught early, and the root cause is addressed, everything stays in balance, alleviating the threat of the Downward Spiral, to remain in a positive and powerful state!

This Awareness method was used by Leila, a Business owner with AuDHD, who felt constantly torn between her business and family. Leila identified that she had invented a new 'doom scrolling' safety mechanism, which took her away from both! In fact, it had started to play out like an addiction, and all areas in her life were suffering, as she procrastinated and avoided the key problems.

By understanding her trigger, she was able to use the skills from the Peace & Power Pathway to reroute her energy. To integrate in her life, rather than feel pressure of letting everyone down. Laila was elated and energised and said that this had allowed her to intertwine both her work and home life, enabling her business to grow, and she became more present with her children.

Integration isn't about balance as in scales. It's about balance as in rhythm. And when your life finds its rhythm, everything changes.

The Ripple Effect

These Five Pillars of The NeuroBrilliant Blueprint are not abstract. They are lived, proven, and powerful. They support moving from browser-tab chaos and burnout spirals to clarity, energy, and impact. Moving on from surviving by someone else's manual - to thriving by writing your own.

And the ripple effect doesn't stop with you. I've seen entrepreneurs escape burnout and grow thriving businesses. Professionals silence their inner critic and step into leadership. Creatives complete pieces of work that changes lives!

When one person rewrites their manual, it doesn't just change their life. It transforms families. Teams. Communities.

It simply starts by using neurodivergent energy and movement, in the right places.

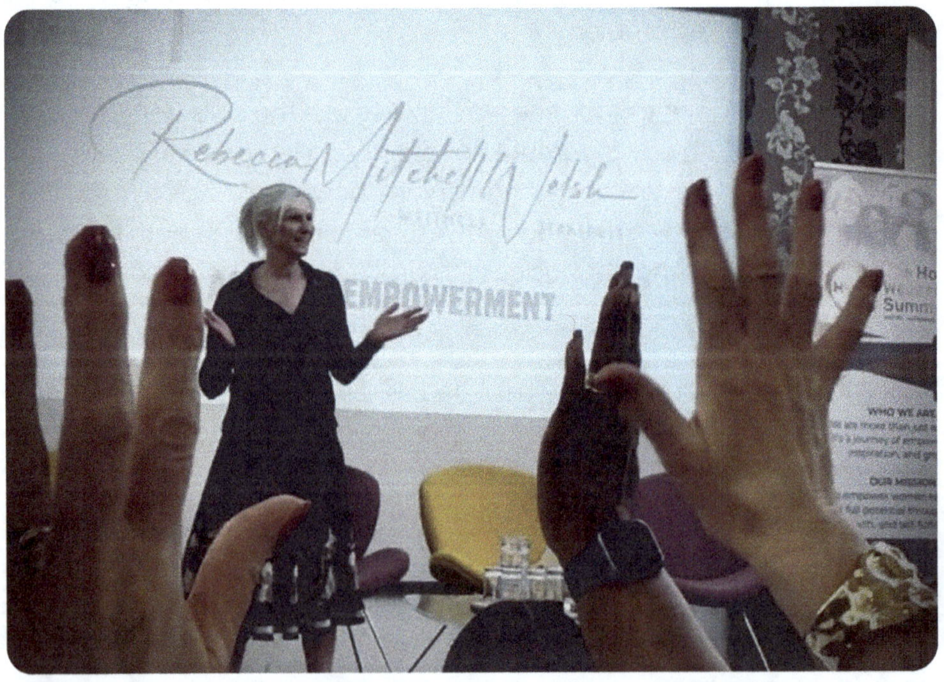

Why Now Is the Time to Act

NeuroBrilliant people have survived years of doing things the hard way, following a map that wasn't written in the right language, being misunderstood and mistreated as a result. And here's the truth, waiting doesn't make change easier. It makes the cost higher.

Women with ADHD are three times more likely to experience anxiety and depression (ADDitude, 2023). Up to 79% of autistic adults report autistic burnout, with women particularly vulnerable due to masking and late diagnosis (Raymaker et al., 2020).

This isn't just stress. It's survival mode. And survival isn't enough for the change-makers the world needs!

Now is the moment to move.
Now is the moment to choose yourself.
Now is the moment to write a new manual, one that finally works for you!

> *"You are exactly who you're meant to be, and with the right strategy, your brilliance can ripple further than you ever imagined."*
>
> **- Rebecca Mitchell Welsh**

REBECCA MITCHELL WELSH

Rebecca is a Wellness and Business Strategist, actively blending her expertise as a number one best-selling author, professional speaker, ACE Mentor and licensed coach to create positive change.

With a specialisation in ADHD, AuDHD, ASD, Dyslexia and Giftedness, she provides tailored strategies that empower neurodiverse entrepreneurs, professionals and creative thinkers to unravel their unique obstacles and leverage their strengths for unparalleled success in professional and personal life.

Her trauma-informed approach and expertise in navigating narcissistic abuse ensure that clients are equipped to overcome personal hurdles and achieve their goals confidently and compassionately.

Rebecca lives on the west coast of Scotland, overlooking the Isle of Arran, and is a proud mum to four actively wonderful children. An advocate for volunteering for lasting impact, Rebecca coaches football locally as a qualified UEFA C Licensed Coach and Talent ID Scout.

**Scan the QR code
for More!**

CONCLUSION

CONCLUSION

The Changemakers:
Entrepreneurs With a Mission, Voices With a Message

As we close this powerful anthology, one truth echoes through every page: **real change begins with one voice, but it never ends there.**

Each of the 17 changemakers you've met in this book began with a spark - a burden, a conviction, or a call for change that refused to be silenced. They faced resistance, fear, and failure, yet they rose and took action - not because the path was easy, but because their purpose was non-negotiable. In choosing to show up, speak up, and stand out, they proved that purpose-driven entrepreneurship is not about self-promotion - it's about transformation.

The Professional Speakers Academy has not merely shaped speakers; it has birthed leaders, reformers, and trailblazers who carry messages that awaken hearts and shift nations. These stories are living proof that when you align your voice with your mission, you create more than success you create significance.

But now, the baton passes to you.

Yes - you, the reader who felt that pull while turning these pages. You who have a message stirring in your spirit, an idea waiting for breath, a dream asking for discipline. This book was never meant to end with applause for others - it was written to activate the changemaker within you.

Because the world doesn't need more noise; it needs more truth.
It doesn't need more competition; it needs more conviction.
It doesn't need more followers; it needs more leaders who serve.
So, take what you've gleaned, guard it, grow it, and go do something with it. Start that business. Share that story. Step onto that stage.

Lead that movement. Become the ripple that someone else's breakthrough depends on. Remember this: you were never called to blend in; you were created to break through and stand out. The changemakers you've read about didn't wait for permission – they answered purpose's call. And now, it's your turn to rise, speak, and serve with the power and authenticity that only you can bring.

Because when one voice awakens, another finds its courage.

And when enough voices rise together – the world shifts.

The Changemakers aren't just in this book. They're in every one of us who dares to believe that our message matters.

Now go.

Be the change.

Your ripple starts here.

Seventeen voices. Seventeen journeys. Seventeen lives that dared to break the mold and say, "I will not settle for ordinary when I am called to extraordinary."

"The world doesn't shift when you dream — it shifts when you decide. Rise, act, and let your life become the evidence that change is possible."

. . .